A to Z of Cricket Terms Explained

ISBN-13: 978-1477696668

ISBN-10: 1477696660

A TO Z OF CRICKET TERMS EXPLAINED

Your Essential Guide to Cricket Terms

Steven Asinni

I dedicate this book to every person – be they man or woman whose lives have been touched by the joy, excitement and sheer fun of cricket...

Cricket...

A sport played by two teams with eleven members each. Known to be rich in its terminology.

But do you know the meaning behind the terms?

I wrote the *A to Z of Cricket Terms Explained* to act as handy glossary of terms. An indispensible reference guide.

Its aim?

To help you get familiar with the sport and appreciate it – through better understanding.

-A-

Across the Line – This term refers to a batsman moving his bat laterally in relation to the ball's direction. As a result of this move, the ball is expected to pitch on the centre or middle stump, at which point the batsman will use his wrists to work the ball around his legs. Not only does this move increase your chance of scoring a run, but it's also quite beautiful to watch.

Agricultural Shot – This move resembles the movement you make with a scythe, which means you simply swing the bat across the ball's line without really using much technique. This shot usually results in the bat digging up part of the pitch. The fact that it resembles a farmer's motion with a scythe is the reason why it's called an agricultural shot.

All Out – This occurs when ten out of the eleven members of the batting team are dismissed, injured, or ill. In this instance, the inning is therefore officially ended. When a batsman is dismissed, he is called "out" and when ten batsmen have been called out, the term "all out" is used although technically, one players remains "not out."

All-rounder – This term refers to a cricket player who plays well at both bowling and batting. Although all cricket bowlers are required to bat as well, most cricket players are adept only at one of these two disciplines. These days, the term is also commonly used to refer to a wicket-keeper who also does very well at batting. The more technically correct term for such a player, though, is wicketkeeper-batsman.

Anchor – This term to a top-calibre batsman who can endure long hours of batting throughout several innings. This type of batsman usually plays third or fourth in the batting line, especially when a batting collapse occurs. Although the main play of an anchor is defensive, he is usually the team's top scorer.

Appeal – This refers to an act where a fielder or bowler yells to confirm with the umpire if the last ball he bowled took the wicket. The commonly shouted terms are "Howzat" (how was that) and "Howzee" (how is he). Sometimes the bowler simply shouts to get the umpire's attention.

Approach – This refers to the movement a bowler makes before he actually bowls the ball. Sometimes this motion is also called a run-up, which is also the term used for the track of ground the fielder runs on. Balance and consistency are two of the principles of making the approach.

Arm Ball – This refers to a strategy where a bowler bowls the ball such that it travels with a backspin, which means the ball goes straight with his arm. If the bowler is particularly good at this strategy, his arm will even swing in the opposite direction from the batsman if he is right-handed or directly towards the batman if the bowler is left-handed. The direction of the ball's travel is where this form of delivery got its name.

Around the Wicket - Also known as Round the Wicket, this term refers to either a right-handed fielder who passes to the right side of the cricket stumps as he bowls or a left-handed fielder who passes to the left. This move is generally described as bowling from the side that places the player's bowling hand far from the stumps. The move doesn't involve any major technical change and is executed purely on "feel."

Ashes – This is the term for the prize in the Test Match Series between Australia and England. This resulted from a satirical obituary in The Sporting Times, which stated that the body of English cricket is to be cremated and its ashes sent to Australia. The obituary was written after the Australian team beat England for the very first time on English ground. When the English team next went to Australia for a match, they dubbed as being on a quest to take back the ashes.

Asking Rate – This term refers to the rate the second team to bat needs to score at so they can catch up with the other team's score during a limited overs match. This is also known as the required run rate. This is often displayed along with the team's actual run rate so viewers will see how well the team is doing.

Attacking Field – This refers to a certain fielding configuration where there are more fielders close to the pitch. The goal is usually for the fielders to dismiss batsmen and take catches more easily. The drawback, however, is that more runs could get scored in the event that the ball gets past the fielders.

Attacking Shot – This term refers to a shot characterized by strength or aggression. It is played to hit sixes and boundaries. The primary aim of such a shot is to score as many runs as possible.

Average – There are actually two types of averages in cricket. The bowler's average is the total runs a bowler concedes divided by the total wickets he takes. The batsman's average is a batsman's total runs scored divided by how many times he was dismissed.

Away Swing – This is a strategy that's considered extremely valuable because it can help a team take wickets. For this reason, fielders who can successfully execute this move are deemed precious assets to any cricket team. Swinging the ball away is also one of the most effective ways of deceiving a batsman.

-B-

Back Foot – For a batman, the foot close to the stumps is called the back foot. For a bowler, it's also known as the bowling foot. The foot of the bowler that comes into contact with the ground last as the ball is released is called the front foot.

Back Foot Contact – This refers to the bowler's position right when the back foot comes into contact with the ground before he delivers the ball. After a run, a bowler typically makes a slight leap in order to gain momentum. He needs to land on his back foot properly after this leap so he can avoid injury and deliver the ball accurately.

Back Foot Shot – This term refers to a shot played by the batsman with his weight on the foot furthest away from the bowler. When you play this shot, it's best to do so with relaxed hands to reduce your chances of being caught near the wickets. You should also remember to keep your front elbow high and the bat faced directly down the wicket.

Back Spin – This is a type of delivery that's also known as under-spin. It is characterised by a backwards rotation. As a result of this rotation, the ball immediately slows down after it is pitched. The ball may also bounce lower as it skids towards the batsman.

Backing Up – This refers to a strategy for shortening the distance in completing a run. A non-striking batsman leaves his crease upon delivery for this purpose. The term also refers to the act of supporting a fielder who receives a throw in case he fails to catch the throw. The risk for a batsman using this strategy is that he could be run out if he back up too far.

Backlift – This refers to the simple act of lifting the bat as a batsman prepares for hitting the ball. Most beginners in the sport make the mistake of lifting the bat too late or lifting it without the right orientation. Always remember to lift the bat while the bowler is still in action and make sure the bat is slanted towards the area between the first and the third slip.

Bail – This refers to one of the pieces of wood located atop the stumps, forming the wicket. It is typically used to identify a broken wicket. The wicket is deemed broken if one or both bails fall or if the ball, the batsman's bat, the striker's body, or the fielder holding the ball strikes a stump off of the ground.

Ball – This term can refer to the physical ball that the batsman strikes with his bat. It is a round, solid, and hard object consisting of cork and covered by leather. It can also refer to a bowler's delivery.

Bang It In – A bowler is said to bang it in when he delivers the ball with added force and speed, and on shorter length. And when he bangs it in, the bowler is also referred to as bending his back. A common mistake players make when banging it in is when they bang it in without enough pace, thus making the ball come down as it approaches the batsman.

Barbecue – This refers to the instance when a poor call results in a batsman running his partner out.

Bat – This refers to the piece of wood used by the batsman in striking the ball. The use of a bat in this sport was first mentioned back in 1624. A cricket bat is typically made of willow.

Bat-pad – This term refers to a fielder who's in the right position to make a catch in case the ball hits the pad right after hitting the bat. The term also refers to the defence commonly used against giving out a batsman lbw. The defence claims that the ball indeed hit the bat before hitting the pad, even if the hit was indiscernible.

Batsman – This is used to refer to a player with batting as his specialty. Specifically, the term refers to the players belonging to the batting team who currently stand at the crease. In women's cricket, the batsman is often called the batter.

Batting – This refers to the act of defending the wicket while scoring runs. Specifically, it refers to the act of hitting the ball with the bat to score a run. The manner in which the ball is hit is referred to as a stroke or shot.

Batting Average – This is the total number of runs a batsman scores per inning, divided by the total number of incidences when the batsman in question was out. This statistic is often used to measure a batsman's performance in a game. The batting average in the sport of baseball is directly descended from cricket's averages.

Batting Collapse – This refers to a situation in a cricket game wherein several batsmen are successively dismissed. This situation can be especially disastrous when it leaves no one but the bowlers to take care of batting. Many defeats in cricket have been blamed on batting collapse.

Batting End – The wickets are typically placed on two ends of the cricket pitch. The term batting end refers to the end or area of the pitch on which the striking batsman stands. This is also the end that's nearest to the wicket keeper.

Batting Order – This term refers to the order followed by the players when they go to bat. Regardless of their specialty, all players in a team need to bat if an inning is completed. The usual batting order follows this pattern: openers (first two batsmen), top order (third and fourth batsmen), middle order (fifth to seventh batsmen), and lower order (eighth to eleventh batsmen).

BBI – This abbreviation refers to the most impressive bowling figures in one inning for the entirety of a bowler's career. It is primarily defined as the most wickets taken and the least runs conceded in an inning. These data are often used in preparing a bowling analysis.

BBM – This abbreviation refers to the most impressive bowling figures in one match for the entirety of a bowler's career. It is primarily defined as the most wickets taken and the least runs conceded in one complete match. The main difference between a BBI and a BBM is that the BBI records statistics for innings whereas BBM records statistics for an entire match.

Beach Cricket – This is an informal version of the sport. As the name suggests, it is basically cricket played on the beach. This form of cricket is particularly popular in Sri Lanka, Australia, and some Caribbean countries.

Beamer – This is a type of delivery wherein the ball approaches the batsman at head height without the need to bounce. It poses a great risk to the batsman, which is why it is deemed an illegal delivery. The usual punishment for this delivery is calling a no ball. In case a bowler delivers over two beamers in a single inning, he may be prohibited from doing any more bowling during that inning.

Beat the Bat – This is a situation where the batsman just narrowly misses hitting the ball with his bat. In this case, the batsman in question is considered as having been beaten and this is often deemed a bowler's moral victory. Sometimes this is expanded and referred to as "beaten all ends."

Beehive – This is a diagram that typically shows where a specific bowler bowled his deliveries in a particular inning. The diagram depicting these deliveries is usually cluster-like, which is how it got its name. This diagram helps people understand the bowler's general pitching areas.

Belter – This refers to a pitch that offers an advantage to the batsman. This kind of pitch is also often described as being a pitch that doesn't offer any assistance or advantage to bowlers. Huge scores are often made on this kind of pitch.

Bend the Back – This refers to the act of making an extra effort to put additional bounce or speed to a delivery. This is often executed by a fast bowler, particularly on a flat pitch. The extra bounce or speed is needed because a flat pitch typically requires some help to bowl.

Bite – This term refers to the turn often produced by a spin bowler on the pitch. The spin bowler is essential to any cricket team, as he can slow the game, attack batsmen, and add pressure to the opposing team. It requires much dedication and lots of practice to be able to execute a consistent bite when spin bowling.

Block – When used as a noun, this term refers to either a defensive shot or the area within the cricket field that contains the pitch. When used as a verb, it refers to the act of playing a defensive shot. The term is also used to describe the position taken by a batsman as he waits for delivery.

Block Hole – This is the area between the batsman's toes and the place where he rests his bat in preparation for receiving a delivery. When the delivery lands in the block hole, it's often called a Yorker. The successful delivery of a Yorker usually forces the batsman to execute a blocking type of shot.

Bodyline – This was a tactic previously used in the sport. It involved bowling right at the body of the batsman. It is also often referred to as "fast leg theory" and is now prohibited by rule changes that restricted fielders to the leg side.

Boot Hill – This is a fielding position that's also known as short leg. It is considered as the most dangerous and least liked of all fielding positions. That's because this position puts the player right in front of the wicket.

Bosie (Bosey) – This is a strategy wherein the ball is bowled as if breaking one way when in fact, it actually breaks the other way. The strategy was named after Bernard Bosanquet, an English cricketer who toured Australia during the summer of 1903 and 1904. The term, however, is now considered obsolete in the sport and the strategy is now referred to as a googly.

Bottom Hand – This refers to the batsman hand that's held closest to the bat's blade. When a shot is played with the batsman's bottom hand, it is usually executed in the air. The bottom hand is usually described as a batsman's dominant hand.

Bouncer – This refers to a fast and short-pitched delivery typically rising close to the batsman's head. This type of delivery is usually executed by fast bowlers. The purpose for pitching it short is to create a bounce that brings the ball to the desired height.

Boundary – This term can refer to any of three things. First, it can refer to the perimeter of a cricket field. Second, the term is also used to refer to four runs. Third, it also refers to the rope demarcating the cricket field's perimeter.

Bowled – This is a form of dismissal afforded to a batsman. This happens when the delivery removes the bails as a result of hitting the stumps. The term can also simply refer to bowling in the past tense.

Bowled Out – When the batting team loses ten of its eleven players, the team is said to have been bowled out. This situation doesn't have anything to do with the type of dismissal referred to as bowled. It simply means the team no longer has any legal batting partnership available.

Bowler – This term refers to the fielding team's player who bowls directly to the batsman. There are generally two types of bowlers in cricket. The pace bowlers are those who rely mostly on ball speed to dismiss a batsman. A spin bowler is one who relies mostly on ball rotation.

Bowling – Simply put, this refers to the act itself of delivering the ball towards the wicket, which is defended by the batsman. Bowling is distinguished from throwing by restrictions as regards the angle at which the bowler's elbow is extended. Bowlers typically deliver in sets consisting of six deliveries, which are collectively referred to as an over.

Bowling Action – This refers to the specific set of movements leading to the release of the ball towards the wicket. As a beginner in the sport, you'll need to analyse your bowling action to make sure it isn't "mixed" because mixed action is a sure way of incurring lower back injuries. Among other things, you need to make sure your hips and shoulders are properly aligned during the bowling action.

Bowl-out – This is a method of deciding a match which would otherwise result in a tie. It is also sometimes called a bowl-off. It involves having five players from each team delivering a ball or two towards an unguarded wicket. If the score is still tied after all ten players have delivered, the bowl-out continues in sudden death style.

Bowling Analysis – This is a statistical notation that summarises a particular bowler's performance. It is also known as bowling figures. A bowling analysis is typically given for every inning in a game or for the entire game. The typical format for a bowling analysis is: Overs Bowled – Number of Overs that are Maidens – Total Runs Conceded – Total Wickets Taken.

Bowling Average – This refers to the figure you get when you divided the total number of runs conceded with the total number of wickets scored. It is defined as the average runs scored off of a particular bowler for every wicket he successfully takes. Therefore, the lower the average is, the better it is for the bowler.

Bowling End – This refers to the part of the pitch where a bowler bowls from. Spin bowlers typically choose the end with rough areas because it helps them achieve the desired bounce and turn. The fast bowler usually chooses the smoother end.

Bowling Foot – This term refers to a bowler's foot that's on the side of his body which is the same as the hand holding the ball. For example, a right-handed bowler's right foot is also his bowling foot.

Box – This is a protective gear that's shaped like half of a shell. It is typically inserted into a jockstrap usually worn underneath the trousers to protect a player's genitalia from being hit by the cricket ball. This piece of protective gear is also called abdominal protector, ball box, or cup.

Brace – This refers to two wickets that are taken during two consecutive deliveries. This instance is also often referred to as being "on a hat trick," since it just one step away from accomplishing a hat trick, which is taking three wickets in three deliveries.

Break – This is typically used to describe a change in direction of the ball after it is pitched, particularly if the change results from a bowler's spin. For example, leg spinners are said to deliver leg breaks, which means the ball moves from the leg side to the off side. The opposite of this delivery is called an off break.

Breaking the Wicket – This term refers to dislodging any of the bails from the wicket stumps. It is mostly used when describing Run Out and Stumping. For example, "The wicket keeper already broke the wicket before the batsman made his ground."

Buffet Bowling – This refers to very poor quality of bowling wherein the batsman could just "help himself" to as many runs as possible. It is also known as Cafeteria Bowling. It is so called because a person can take whatever food they want in large amounts when they eat at a buffet.

Bump Ball – This is a type of delivery wherein the ball bounces very near the batsman's foot right after a shot is played that it would seem to come directly off the bat without hitting the ground. A crowd catch often results from such a delivery. Spectators who don't see the bounce will often assume the batsman is out in case the ball is caught.

Bumper – This is the old-fashioned name for bouncer, which is a delivery often bowled by fast bowlers. This delivery is executed such that the ball bounces well short of the batsman. A bumper is generally considered tactically effective in the game of cricket.

Bunny – This term refers to a team member who bats at the eleventh spot almost all the time. This player is typically designated as wicketkeeper or a specialist bowler. He is also known as Rabbit.

Bunsen – This term refers to a type of pitch where a spin bowler can prodigiously turn the ball. The term is taken from "Bunsen burner," which cricketers have made into a slang that means "turner." The word is often used by game commentators.

Bye – This refers to extras that are scored just like a normal run where the ball makes no contact with the batsman or his bat. Normally, the wicketkeeper will catch a ball that passes the batsman without being hit. But, if the wicketkeeper fails to catch the ball, the batsman could safely score runs. These runs will then be added to the team's score, but not to the batsman's individual score.

-C-

Call – This refers to the act of shouting "Mine!" This is done by a fieldsman to let other fieldsmen know he's in the right position to make a catch. The term also refers to a batsman's act of announcing to his partner whether they will take a run or not. A batsman will usually shout Yes, No, or Wait to call a play.

Called – This refers to an instance when the umpire calls a no-ball. This call is usually made after a bowler makes an illegal delivery. It results in a run or two being added to the score of the batting team.

Cameo – This refers to a brief and quick-scoring inning. This type of inning is typically played by a middle order or lower order batsman. When a batsman accomplishes this, he is said to have played "a cameo of an inning."

Cap – This refers to an award given by countries for every appearance of a player at Test level. One is given at county level, but it isn't given on the player's first appearance. Rather, it is awarded when the player has proven himself as a team member. There are players who never receive a cap.

Captain's Knock/Captain's Innings – This refers to an instance when a high-scoring inning of the batting team's captain is deemed to have significantly changed a game's course. The term gets its name from the sound (knock) of the bat hitting the ball. It is now used in other sports as well to indicate a team captain's performance, which helps the team win the game.

Carom Ball – This is a bowling delivery style that got its name from the fact that the ball is flicked between the bowler's thumb and middle finger. The middle finger is bent so as to create a spin in the delivery. The style is said to have originated in the 1940s, but it was once again popularized in the 2000s by a player named Ajantha Mendis.

Carry – This refers to an instance when a fielder catches a hit ball on the fly. If the ball bounces before the fielder catches it, then it has not carried. The term also refers to a measure of pitch quality.

Carry the Bat – This refers to an opening batsman who is still not out by the time an inning is completed. However, the term is commonly used only when the inning is closed after the ten other players of the team are dismissed. The term originally referred to any batsman who is not out by the end of an inning, but it became exclusively used in reference to an opener by the 20th century.

Cart-wheeling Stump – This refers to an instance when the stump is hit so forcefully that it revolves vertically before landing on the ground. A stump usually goes cart-wheeling when the ball hits the top part at considerable speed. It's a fast bowler's dream to see a batsman's stump cartwheel off his bowling.

Castled – This refers to being out-bowled by either a Yorker or full-length ball. This is also known as an unplayable ball for a batsman. When this happens, the batsman is said to have been castled.

Catch – This refers to the act of dismissing a batsman because a fielder catches the ball after it was hit but before it lands on the ground. This is said to be the most common way a batsman is dismissed at higher competition levels. Any runs scored off the delivery where the batsman is caught will be voided.

Caught and Bowled – This refers to a player getting dismissed as a result of a bowler's catch. The term is taken from the manner in which the dismissal is recorded on the scorecard. The chronological description, bowled and caught, is very seldom used.

Caught Behind – This term refers to the catch made by the wicket-keeper. This results in the dismissal of the batsman. Caught behind is actually an unofficial but generally accepted term in cricket.

Centurion – This term refers to a cricketer who scores over a hundred runs in a single inning. The honour of being the very first cricket centurion is given to John Minshull, who scored over a hundred in a game played in 1769. The first batsman to become a centurion more than a hundred times is W. G. Grace, who reached this milestone in 1895.

Century – This term refers to an individual batsman's score of a hundred runs or more. The term is also sometimes used to refer to a bowler who concedes over a hundred runs in a single inning. When batting partners score a hundred runs together, it is called a century partnership.

Charge – This refers to a batsman's act of using his feet and coming out of his crease, moving towards the bowler in an attempt at hitting the ball. It is also referred to as stepping down the wicket. A batsman doing this is also said to be giving the charge to the bowler.

Cherry – This term refers to the cricket ball, the new one in particular. It can also refer to the red marks the ball leaves on a bat. The term is taken from the bright cherry red color of the ball.

Chest On – This term refers to a bowler whose chest and hips are aligned towards the direction of the batsman upon back foot contact. This is the position a bowler takes as his back foot makes contact with the ground prior to ball delivery. In the same way, a batsman with hips and shoulders facing the bowler is referred to as being chest on.

Chin Music – This term is taken from the sport of baseball. It refers to the act of using several bouncers to intimidate the batsman. In the history of cricket, this strategy was commonly used against sub-continental teams who lacked experience with bouncers.

Chinaman – This term refers to left-handed bowlers who bowl wrist spin. In this case, you're likely to notice the ball moving from the left to the right side of your TV screen. The term traces its origins to Ellis Achong, a left-handed Chinese bowler who played for a West Indian team.

Chinese Cut – This refers to an inside edge that fails to hit the stumps by just a few centimetres. This usually happens when the batsman attempts to execute an attacking shot. Other terms that mean the same thing are Surrey Cut, Harrow Drive, and French Cut.

Chuck – This term refers to the act of throwing, rather than bowling, the ball. This happens when the bowler's elbow straightens during delivery. This is considered an illegal action and generally implies cheating.

Circle – This refers to the painted circle at the centre of the pitch. The circle has a radius of 30 yards. It separates the outfield from the infield and is generally used to police fielding regulations in one-day cricket games. The restrictions may vary according to the game type.

Clean Bowled – This term means the ball is bowled and the wicket is broken without the ball hitting the pad or bat. This is also sometimes defined as the batsman having missed the ball, resulting to the ball hitting the stumps. When this happens, the batsman is said to have been beaten by the ball.

Close Infield – This refers to the area that's enclosed by the painted circle with a radius of 15 yards. The area is measured on both ends of the pitch. This is used solely for ODI matches.

Coil – This term means the same thing as back foot contact. To avoid injury, a player should remember to align his hips and shoulders at the coil. The right foot is normally the back foot of a right-handed bowler and the left foot for a left-handed bowler.

Collapse – This refers to losing a number of wickets within a short period of time. A team that fails to successfully guard their wickets within a very short time, thus resulting to a number of runs, is therefore said to have collapsed.

Come to the Crease – This phrase is commonly used to refer to a batsman who walks onto the playing field and arrives at the pitch to start batting. The batting crease is the area where the batsman is restricted and legally allowed to hit the ball from. When the batsman approaches the crease, he is expected to be ready to bat.

Contrived Circumstances – This term refers to unusual tactics used by a team with the intent of achieving a legitimate outcome. The result of the tactic, however, involves wild statistical abnormalities. An example of such tactic is when a bowler deliberately bowls poorly to get a quick declaration.

Cordon – This is a collective term that refers to all fielders positioned behind the batsman. These fielders are typically positioned that way to catch an edged ball that's beyond the wicket-keeper's reach. A cordon is generally farther than the wicket-keeper from the batsman.

Corridor of Uncertainty – This refers to a narrow area just outside the off stump of a batsman. If a delivery goes into this area, the batsman can have a bit of difficulty deciding whether to play defensively, execute an attacking shot, or leave the ball. This phrase was popularised by Geoffrey Boycott, a former batsman of an English team.

County Cricket – This is the highest of all domestic cricket levels in Wales and England. The main English cricket teams are the eighteen first-class counties. These teams were originally represented and are named after the historic English counties.

Covers – This refers to a fielding position that's between mid-off and point. The term is also used to refer to the equipment that protects the cricket pitch from rain. Cricket covers are usually tarpaulins.

Cow Corner – This refers to the field area between the wide long-on and the deep mid-wicket. The area is named as such because only a few shots are aimed towards this area. Fielders are therefore seldom positioned in the area, thus giving rise to comments that cows can freely graze in that part of the cricket field.

Cow Shot – This refers to a hard shot that aims to hit the cricket ball beyond the boundary at the cow corner. This is a very powerful shot and often an excellent way of achieving boundary sixes. However, it has to be perfectly timed to avoid being caught or bowled.

Crease – This term refers to any one of the lines on the cricket pitch that are near the stumps. The term is most often used in reference to the popping crease. The term may also refer to the area demarcated by painted or chalked white lines.

Cricket Ball – This is a hard and solid ball made of cork and wound string and then covered by polished leather. It has a wide and raised equatorial seam. Cricket law heavily regulates the manufacture of this ball.

Cricketer – This term is used in reference to a cricket player. Each cricketer plays a specific role in the team. There are also cricketers who are skilled in both bowling and batting, and these players are called all-rounders.

Cross-bat Shot – This refers to a shot executed with the bat held parallel to the ground. Such a shot is also called a horizontal-bat shot. Common examples of this shot are the cut and the pull.

Crowd Catch – This refers to a fielder's stop that causes the crowd to roar. The reason for the roar is that the usual first impression is that the stop is a dismissal. However, due to a bump ball or no ball, it's actually not a dismissal.

Cut – This refers to a shot executed at a short-pitched ball, thus placing it wide off stump. In this case, the batsman typically makes little effort as he diverts the ball using the bowler's pace. The shot is so-called because of the cutting motion the batsman makes upon executing the shot.

Cutter – This refers to a break delivery that's bowled by either a fast bowler or a medium-pace bowler. The action is similar to that of a spin bowler, but the pace is faster. The aim of this delivery is usually to catch the batsman by surprise.

-D-

Daisy Cutter – This refers to an instance when the cricket ball bounces more than twice or rolls along the cricket pitch before it reaches the batsman. The term is also defined as a ball that's bowled in a manner that lets it stay very near the ground. Any low-flying ball in cricket is therefore called a daisy cutter.

Dead Ball – This refers to the part of a cricket game in between deliveries, wherein batsmen aren't allowed to score runs and cannot be given out. Dead ball is also called whenever the cricket ball gets lodged in a batsman's equipment or clothing. The term also refers to an instance when the cricket ball is bowled but the batsman isn't ready yet. It also refers to an instance when a bowler ends a run up without a delivery.

Dead Bat – This refers to an instance when the bat is held in such a light grip that it gives as it hits the ball. This results in the ball losing momentum and falling to the ground. When a batsman does this, he is said to have played with a dead bat.

Death Overs – This refers to the last ten overs in a single-day match. This is when most bowlers are typically hit for a lot of runs. Players who bowl at this time are referred to as "bowling at the death." Another term for this is Slog Overs.

Death Rattle – This is the sound typically heard by a batsman as a result of being clean bowled. It is so-called in reference to the gurgling sound a person makes as he is about to die.

Decision Review System – This refers to a new technology-based system that was first used in Test Cricket. The main purpose of this system is to review controversial decisions that may be made by on-field umpires. The system was officially launched in November 2009.

Declaration – This refers to a team captain voluntarily closing his team's innings. This is usually done when the captain believes his team's score is good enough to guarantee a win. It is most commonly done in timed matches so that the team will have adequate time to bowl out the opposing team and secure the win.

Declaration Bowling – This phrase is generally used in reference to deliberately poor bowling. This is usually done by the fielding team so the batsman can quickly score runs and the batting team's captain will declare. Examples of deliberately poor bowling are long hops and full tosses.

Defensive Field – This refers to a fielding configuration wherein the fielders are spread across the field. The aim is to reduce runs scored by batsmen and stop hit balls readily. The drawback, however, is that the fielding team will have fewer chances to make catches or dismiss batsmen.

Delivery – This refers to the actual bowling of the ball. A player from the fielding team is assigned to bowl for one over, after which another team member takes over. Six consecutive bowls constitute an over.

Devil's Number – This refers to the number 87, which is considered unlucky by Australian cricketers. It is also known as the Dreaded Number and teams typically don't want to get such a score. The superstition is said to have originated from the fact that the number is just 13 runs short of achieving a century. Australian teams also claim that batsmen usually get dismissed for 87.

Diamond Duck – This refers to either a dismissal off an inning's first ball or getting dismissed without facing delivery. These instances are also sometimes referred to as Platinum Duck. The usage of the term varies from one region to the next.

Dibbly Dobbly – This term refers to a bowler who has limited skills. It can also refer to a delivery that's very easy to hit. Dibbly dobblers are often used in a game as a gamble.

Dilscoop – This refers to a stroke wherein the batsman goes down on one knee, then hits the ball with a good length over the head of the wicket-keeper and beyond the boundary. The stroke was named after Sri Lankan player Tillakaratne Dilshan, who displayed it at the ICC World 20 in 2009. The stroke is also a known specialty of the New Zealand cricketer Brendon McCullum.

Dink – This term refers to a shot executed in a gentle way. The term is also used as a verb, which means to hit the ball gently. In other sports, this is also known as a drop shot.

Dipper – This term refers to a delivery that curves away from or towards the batsman before it pitches. Strictly speaking, a dipper isn't a type of delivery, but part of a seaming, cutting, or swinging delivery. It is so-called because of its dipping nature.

Dismiss – This refers to the act of getting a batsman out so he is required to stop batting. When the bowling team has dismissed ten of the eleven batsmen, it is said to have bowled out the entire batting team. This is because batsmen are required to bat in pairs, so when there's only one batsman left, he may no longer bat.

Direct Hit – This refers to a deep fieldsman's throw that directly brings a wicket down. A deep fieldsman's throw is usually caught by the fieldsman positioned at the stumps before it is thrown to strike the wicket. A direct hit typically occurs when an attempt at a run out is made.

Dolly – This term refers to an extremely easy catch. The term is said to have originated from the Anglo-Indian term that literally means a friendly offer of food. When the batsman hits a dolly, it's as if he is offering the ball to the fieldsmen.

Donkey Drop – This term refers to a ball that has an extremely high trajectory before it bounces. The term may also be used in reference to a style of bowling known as lob bowling. This was very common in the 19th century, when trajectory was a very important consideration in the game.

Doosra – This refers to a new type of off spin delivery that was introduced by Saqlain Mushtaq. It is known as the finger spin version of the googly because it is said to turn the wrong way. The term was first heard from Moin Khan, a Pakistani wicket-keeper.

Dot Ball – This refers to a delivery off of which no runs are scored. It got its name from the fact that such a delivery is recorded in score books with a dot. The most common reason for the absence of runs is that the batsmen simply decided to defend rather than attack.

Double – This term normally refers to the scoring of a thousand runs as well as the taking of a hundred wickets in a single season. This is an extremely rare feat outside of England due to fewer first-class matches in other countries. Even in England, the feat isn't all that common, the last double having been achieved back in 1988 by Franklyn Stephenson.

Double Hat-trick – This refers to the act of taking four wickets within four consecutive balls. The only international cricketer to ever achieve this feat is Sri Lankan Lasith Malinga. And the only cricketer to have achieved this along with a century in a single match is Hampshire cricketer Kevan James.

Down the Pitch – This term describes a batsman's motion towards the bowler before or during a delivery. It is typically made with the aim of taking a good length ball and turning it into a half-volley. Another term for the move is Down the Wicket.

Draw – This term refers to a result wherein the last team to bat aren't all out, but they fail to surpass the opposing team's score in a timed match. This shouldn't be confused with a tie, wherein the last team to bat is all out and the scores are level. The term could also refer to an antiquated stroke wherein the ball is played between a player's legs.

Draw Stumps – This refers to the act of declaring the game over. It could also be a reference to the drawing of the stumps out of the ground by the umpire, thus terminating the game.

Drift – This term refers to the slightly lateral movement a spinner extracts as the cricket ball is still in flight. Being able to achieve this is considered as very good bowling. A late drift often results in the batsman covering the wrong line, thus the ball is likely to catch the bat's edge.

Drinks – This refers to a brief break in the play. This break is usually taken towards the middle of the session. It is so called because refreshments are typically brought to the umpires and players. Such breaks usually happen in hot countries.

Drinks Waiter – This term is typically used to refer to the twelfth man on a team. Part of the job of the twelfth man is to bring out the refreshments during a drinks break. The term is often used in jest.

Drive – This refers to a powerful shot that's generally hit close to the ground. Sometimes it is also hit into the air, particularly in a direction towards the area between the cover point and mid-wicket. The shot may also be hit in an arc about thirty degrees on each side along the pitch.

Drop – This can refer to accidentally dropping a ball initially caught by the fielder, thus failing to dismiss the batsman. When this happens, it is said that the batsman has been dropped. The term may also refer to the total number of dismissals that happen in an inning before a particular batsman goes in. The third batsman is said to be batting at first drop.

Drop-in Pitch – This refers to a temporary pitch typically cultivated off-site. This allows a number of different sports to share in the use of the same field while minimising the risk of injury to players. It is so called because the pitch is literally dropped into the field for a game of cricket.

DRS – This is a common abbreviation that refers to the Decision Review System. The system itself has a dramatic impact on cricket. Because of this, the system is now also under review.

Duck – This refers to the score of a batsman that's known as zero dismissed. When this happens, the batsman is said to be "out for a duck." The original term was "duck's egg" due to the O shape recorded in the scorebook.

Duck under Delivery – This refers to a delivery that looks like a bouncer, thus making a striker duck so as not to get hit. But, rather than bouncing high, the ball bounces low and causes the dismissal of the batsman with an LBW.

Duckworth-Lewis Method – This is a math-based rule, which sets a specific target score for the team that bats second in a single-day match affected by rain. It is said to be the most accurate way to set a target score. The method was devised by English statisticians Tony Lewis and Frank Duckworth.

-E-

Eagle-eye – This refers to a computer system that's used to track the ball's trajectory and record the path it's likely to take. It was developed in 2001 and is now a part of cricket's adjudication process. The system is based on principles of triangulation and uses visual images.

Economical – This refers to a bowler conceding only a very few runs. The opposite of this type of bowler is called expensive. An economical bowler is said to have a very low economy rate.

Economy Rate – This term refers to the average amount of runs scored in each over. The equation to get this statistic is ER = runs/overs bowled. This is included in the record of a bowler's statistics.

Edge – This refers to a slight deviation made by the cricket ball off of the bat's edge. This deviation may be an inside, outside, top, or bottom edge, depending on whether the bat is held vertical or horizontal. This is also known as a nick or snick.

Eleven – This is another term for a cricket team. The term was coined in reference to the fact that a team is comprised of eleven players. Though each player in a team has a specialty, they each take their turn at batting.

End – This refers to an area directly behind a stump that's used to designate the end from where the bowler will bowl. Cricket bowlers are required to take turns bowling the opposite ends of the cricket pitch. If the bowler bowls from the side of the field where you find the pavilion, then that's called the pavilion end.

Expensive – This is the opposite of economical. It refers to a bowler conceding plenty of runs. He is said to have high economy rate.

Extra – This refers to a run that's not attributed to a batsman. The five types of extras are penalties, byes, leg byes, no-balls, and wides. The first three are collectively called fielding extras and the other two are known as bowling extras.

-F-

Fall – This is a verb that indicates a batsman's dismissal. For example, "The sixth wicket fell..." The mechanics of dismissal are discussed in Laws 27 to 29 of the Laws of Cricket.

Fall of Wicket – This refers to the score of the batting team at the point when a batsman is dismissed. In scorecards, you'll often see this abbreviated to FoW. An example of the term's usage is, "The second fall of wicket is 300 runs."

Farm the Strike – This refers to the act of a batsman of deliberately scoring runs or declining to take runs so that one batsman receives a majority of balls bowled. It is typically the more skilled batsman that's chosen to face more balls. This is also known as Farm the Bowling or Shepherd the Strike.

Fast Bowling – This refers to a bowling style wherein the ball is bowled at high speed, usually over 90mph. It is also known as pace bowling. Along with spin bowling, this is one of the main approaches to cricket bowling.

Fast Leg Theory – This is a variant of the leg theory, which refers to balls being fast bowled and aimed at the body of the batsman. This tactic was devised by the team from England for the 1932-33 Ashes Tour. The aim was to combat the excellent batting skills of Don Bradman, an Australian batsman.

Feather – This term refers to a faint edge. This occurs when the batsman makes an attempt to hit the ball, but only succeeds in making a slight contact with the bat. It's also sometimes called a snick.

Featherbed – This refers to a wicket that's considered good for batting, as it offers little or no help to the bowler. This is also used to describe a pitch that's soft and flat, and is characterised by a predictable bounce and slow pace, which makes batting very easy. Such a pitch is definitely very tough for the bowler.

Ferret – This term refers to a batsman who's performance is even poorer than that of a rabbit. The term was coined because ferrets normally go in after rabbits. Another term for such a batsman is weasel.

Fielder – This term refers to a cricketer belonging to the fielding team who neither bowls nor guards the wicket. More specifically, it refers to a player who just fielded a ball. The main responsibility of such a player is to get the ball after it is hit by the batsman. His goal is to either prevent the batsman from scoring runs or to catch him out.

Fill-Up Game – This refers to a time when a cricket match finishes early and another game is started in order to fill the remaining time and entertain the spectators. The term also refers to the actual game that's started when the main match finishes ahead of time. These were unofficial games that were played just for fun.

Find the Gap – This refers to the act of playing a shot or several shots between fielders, close to the ground. This is identified as the least risky manner of quickly scoring runs. However, a player needs to have excellent technique to accomplish it consistently.

Fine – This refers to the position opposite of square. The term describes a certain position or location on the field near or on the line that runs down the pitch's length and through both wickets. This position is usually behind the batsman.

First Change – This refers to the third bowler in an inning. Being the first player to replace one of the opening bowlers, this is therefore the first change a team captain makes to their attack.

First-Class Cricket – This refers to the senior version of the sport, usually at the level of state, county, or international. Matches at these levels typically have two innings for each side. These matches are usually played in three days or more. Although Test Cricket is considered as the highest cricket standard, it is still technically classified as first-class cricket.

First Innings Points – This refers to the points awarded to a team for taking a lead in the first innings. These points are typically awarded in first-class cricket matches where a league table is used to determine standings. They are in addition to the points given for winning a game or securing a tie.

Fishing – This term refers to the act of being tempted to throw the bat at an outside off-stump wide delivery. Simply put, it describes the act of reaching for and missing a wide delivery. A batsman who does this is said to have gone fishing after the ball.

Five-Wicket Haul – This is another term for five-fer of fifer. It describes a bowler's feat of taking at least five wickets in a single inning. It is also colloquially known as Michelle.

Flash – This refers to the act of wielding the bat aggressively. This often results in indiscriminately hitting good length and line deliveries.

Flat Throw – This refers to a ball which, when thrown by a fielder, flies almost completely parallel to the ground. This type of throw travels very fast and if the fielder also throws it accurately, then it is considered as a hallmark of excellent fielding. Fielders who cannot throw fast and flat could easily lose their spot in a team.

Flat-track Bully – This term refers to a batsman who performs really well only when the bowlers do not get much assistance from the pitch. Nevertheless, this batsman is typically ranked high in the team's batting order. The term comes from the fact that a pitch that offers little to no assistance to bowlers is called a flat pitch.

Flick – This refers to the act of moving the bat with a gentle wrist movement. The movement is usually associated with leg side shots. The term may also refer to the act of a bowler turning his wrist to achieve a leg spin.

Flight – This term refers to a delivery that's given an arched trajectory by the spinner. This is considered as an excellent way to bowl. The strategy is also known as a loop.

Flipper – This term refers to a leg spin that also has an under-spin. As a result, the ball bounces much lower than normal. This type of delivery is said to have been invented by cricketer Clarrie Grimmett.

Floater – This term refers to a spinner's delivery that follows an arched path and appears to float up in the air. This delivery is typically done by an off spinner. It is characterised by the ball curving away from a right-handed batsman and then, instead of turning, it carries straight on.

Fly Slip – This term refers to a position that's deeper than conventional slips. This is typically an area between the third man and the slips. The position belongs to the catching positions of cricket fielding.

Follow On – This refers to the team batting first during the second inning after batting second during the first inning. If the team batting first during the first inning leads by a considerable margin after the inning, the team captain may direct the second batting team to follow on. This margin is usually 150 runs for a three-day game or 200 runs for a five-day game.

Follow Through – This term refers to a bowler's actions to stabilise his body after releasing the ball. When he follows through, a bowler will typically continue running a few steps once the ball is released. To avoid entering the danger area, will usually turn towards the opposite direction of the pitch.

Footmarks – This term describes the rough patches created by a bowler on grass pitches. These patches are typically created where the bowler's foot lands when he delivers the ball. Spin bowlers usually aim the ball at these rough patches to give it a sharper turn, thus making it harder for the batsmen to hit.

Footwork – This refers to the steps a batsman needs to take to reach a good distance from the point where the ball pitched. The distance has to be just right so the batsman can hit it wherever he wants, thus negating any swing or spin the bowler may have extracted after bouncing. This is also simply defined as the movement made by the batsman's feet when he prepares to evade or hit the ball.

Forty-five – This is a fielding position that's not very commonly seen in the game. It is similar to the short third man. The area is about halfway between the boundary and the pitch. The term may also be used to describe a position about 45 degrees behind square.

Forward Defence – This refers to a defensive shot that's commonly used in a game. The batsman executes this shot by smothering the cricket ball before it can spin. The shot may also be used to combat variable bounce, particularly when the batsman bends his front knee when making the shot.

Four – This term refers to a shot which, after the ball touches the ground, reaches the boundary and scores four runs for the batting team. Whenever this happens, the ball automatically becomes dead. If the ball didn't touch the batsman or the bat, then the four will be scored as an extra.

Four Wickets – This term refers to an instance when a bowler takes at least four wickets in a single inning. This is most commonly used in one-day international matches. This feat is generally considered as a very good performance from a bowler.

Free Hit – This refers to a penalty that's given in some cricket games as a result of a bowler delivering front foot no-balls. The bowler will then have to bowl again and the batsman is safe from dismissal in that delivery. Fielders aren't allowed to change positions at this time unless the batsmen themselves changed ends.

French Cricket – This refers to an informal version of the game. There's only one batsman in this game and his only objective is not to get dismissed. The term may also be used by game commentators in reference to a batsman who hasn't moved his feet, thus looking ungainly as a result.

French Cut – This term refers to the inside edge that misses the stumps only by a number of centimetres. This is usually an accidental shot that occurs when the batsman attempts to block or drive the ball. This is also known as a Surrey Cut, Harrow Drive, or Chinese Cut.

Front Foot – For a batsman, this refers to the foot that's positioned closer to the bowler. For a bowler, this refers to the foot that makes contact with the ground last prior to the release of the ball. This is also known as the batsman's non-dominant foot.

Front Foot Contact – This refers to the bowler's position as his front foot touches the ground just before the ball is delivered. Bowlers usually make a small leap to gain momentum after a run. He will need to properly land first on his back foot , then on his front foot to avoid injury and correctly deliver the ball. Right-handed bowlers typically use their left foot as the front foot.

Front Foot Shot – This term refers to a shot executed by the batsman with his weight mostly on the front foot. A batsman naturally tries to transfer his weight to his front foot so he can play fuller length deliveries. Generally, fuller length and good length deliveries are both played with a front foot shot.

Fruit Salad – This refers to a bowler executing a different style of delivery every time instead of bowling with the same length, speed, and angle. This is most commonly used in T20's for purposes of not allowing the batsmen to get comfortable. A fruit salad keeps the batsmen guessing as regards what to expect from the bowler.

Full Length – This refers to a ball delivery that pitches much closer than a good length delivery, but farther than a half-volley. The main purpose of such a delivery is to deceive the batsman. This type of delivery is also known as a Yorker.

Full Toss – This refers to a delivery wherein the ball doesn't bounce before it reaches the batsman. This is considered as bad delivery because it gives the batsman plenty of opportunity to execute an attacking shot. This type of delivery also doesn't give the ball any chance of changing direction, thus being considered as a spin bowler's ultimate crime.

-G-

Gardening – This refers to a batsman who prods at the pitch using his bat in-between deliveries. A batsman typically does this to flatten a bump, to upset the bowler's rhythm, to soothe his nerves, or to simply waste time. This is generally considered facetious, since there really isn't any point to the action.

Gazunder – This is an Australian term that describes a delivery wherein the ball fails to reach the desired height after it bounces. As a result, the delivery beats the batsman as it "goes under" his bat. This delivery often achieves the result of the batsman being out bowled.

Getting Your Eye In – This refers to a batsman's act of taking the time to evaluate the condition of the ball, weather, and pitch before attempting some potentially risky strokes. It is generally believed that such an exercise helps improve a batsman's timing, which is very important for successful batting. This is considered very important because batting is all about good footwork and hand-to-eye coordination.

Given Man – This refers to players in cricket's early history who normally didn't play for a specific team, but were included in the roster to strengthen the team. First-class cricket matches used to be subject to huge wagers, which is why it was important for both teams to be perceived as having roughly equal strength. This is a similar concept to handicapping in horse racing, where horses are made to carry different weights to give them equal chances of winning.

Glance – This term refers to a shot executed in a very fine manner behind the batsman, usually at leg side. This shot is usually played on short-pitched balls. It requires some wrist work, as the ball is flicked with the bat and deflected towards the fine leg area.

Glove – This is an important part of the batsman's kit. It protects the batsman's hands from injury. A hand holding a bat is considered one with the bat. Therefore, a batsman may be given out when he is caught to a ball coming off his glove. In this case, he is said to have gloved a catch.

Glovemanship – This refers to the act of wicket-keeping. It is also known as Gauntlet Work. When a wicket-keeper delivers a good performance, he is said to have displayed marvellous glovemanship.

Golden Duck – This term refers to dismissals for nought from the very first ball a batsman faces in their side's innings. The term "duck" is generally used in reference to a batsman's zero score. It is so called because of the resemblance between the zero figure and a duck's egg.

Golden Pair – This term refers to dismissals for nought off the very first ball a batsman faced in each of their team's two innings in a two-innings match. This is also known as a King Pair. Any batsman who suffers from such a dismissal is said to have suffered the indignity of a king pair.

Good Length – This refers to the ideal pitching area of a stock delivery as it moves from bowler to batsman. This usually makes a batsman unsure as to whether he should play a back-foot or front-foot shot. This isn't necessarily the ideal length to bowl, since different batsmen have different weaknesses and different lengths are needed to exploit those weaknesses.

Googly – This term refers to a deceptive delivery executed by leg spin bowlers. For right-handed bowlers and batsmen, a googly typically turns from off side to leg side. This was formerly called a bosey or bosie. In Australia, it is called the wrong 'un.

Gouging – This term refers to the act of deliberately causing damage to the ball or pitch. This can be considered as misconduct and penalised by the umpire. Needless to say, gouging is highly discouraged.

Grafting – This term refers to the act of batting defensively, usually under difficult conditions. The main focus of this batting style is placed on not getting out.

Green Top – This refers to a pitch that has an unusual amount of grass. This is usually expected to provide assistance to pace bowlers. The visibly green grass indicates significant moisture, which causes unpredictable bounce in fast-bowled balls, thus making it more difficult to bat.

Grip – This refers to the rubber casings on the bat's handle. The term may also be used to describe the way a bowler holds the cricket ball and the way a batsman holds his bat. A bowler can usually generate pace or spin simply by varying his grip.

Groundsman – This term refers to the person responsible for the maintenance of the cricket field. This person is also responsible for preparing the pitch for a match. There are a number of seminars and courses provided to those who wish to become cricket groundsmen.

Grubber – This term refers to a delivery that almost has no bounce. The ball flies off the pitch at an unusually low level that it's very difficult for a batsman to successfully play at it. Sometimes a grubber simply rolls along the ground.

Guard – This refers to a batsman's act of aligning his bat with a chosen stump behind him. A batsman typically marks his bat's position on the pitch. This gives him an idea as regards where he stands relative to the stumps.

Gully – This refers to a fielder positioned close to the slip fielders, particularly at an angle of about 100-140 degrees between the stumps. The position is designed for catching a ball that was deflected a long way. The term is also used to refer to that particular area where the fielder is positioned.

Gun Bowler – This term refers to a team's principal attacking bowler. The term is also sometimes used in ten-pin bowling.

-H-

Hack – This term refers to a batsman who approaches batting very aggressively despite a generally low skill level. This type of batsman generally prefers lofted cross-bat shots. Other features of this type of batsman are the absence of defensive strokes and poor defensive stance. The term is also used to describe a particular stroke.

Half Century – This term refers to a batsman's score of more than 50 but less than 100. This is a significant landmark for any batsman, but more so for a lower order batsman and a tail-ender. The term can also refer to fifty runs scored together by a pair of batsmen.

Half-tracker – This is another term used in reference to a long hop. It is so called due to the fact that the ball bounces about halfway down the cricket pitch. When delivered by a slow bowler, this is considered poor delivery because the batsman is likely to hit it to the boundary.

Half-volley – This term refers to a delivery, which bounces short of a block hole. This delivery is usually easy to glance or drive away. This is also defined as a delivery executed such that the batsman is easily able to hit the ball as it bounces off the pitch. The term is also used to refer to the act of hitting the ball immediately after it bounces.

Half Yorker – This refers to a delivery that's deliberately bowled right at the stumps' base. It is also defined as an over-pitched Yorker and a delivery similar to a half-volley. When a bowler misses the area within which the perfect Yorker should land, he is said to have bowled a Half Yorker.

Harrow Drive – This refers to a shot misplayed by the batsman. As a result, the ball comes off the bat's inside edge and then narrowly misses the stumps. The shot typically goes to fine leg. It is also known as French Cut or Chinese Cut.

Hat-trick – This refers to a bowler's feat of taking a wicket off of each of his three consecutive deliveries in the same match. It doesn't matter if this happens within a single over or within two consecutive overs. It may even happen in the last over of one inning and the first over of the next inning.

Hat-trick Ball – This refers to a delivery that's bowled after two wickets are taken in the two previous deliveries. The team captain will typically maximise a bowler's chances of taking a hat-trick by setting an attacking field.

Hawk-Eye – This refers to computer-generated graphics that show a ball's probable trajectory if the batsman doesn't hinder it. This is officially used by the game's third umpire for purposes of assessing lbw decisions as part of the DRS. Game commentators may also use it to assess a bowler's deliveries.

Have the Call – This term refers to a batsman's responsibility of announcing to his partner whether to take a run or not. Generally accepted practice requires the batsman with better view to make the call. There are times, however, when partners agree that the batsman with more experience should always be the one to have the call.

Heavy Roller – This term refers to a very heavy metal cylinder used by ground staff for purposes of improving a wicket. Specifically, it is rolled onto the pitch in order to flatten it. According to the laws of cricket, the batting team's captain gets to decide whether the heavy or light roller will be used between innings.

Helicopter Shot – This refers to a stroke that's executed by swinging the cricket bat such that it hits the ball in part from below. The motion is similar to an uppercut and the angle followed by the bat typically exceeds 180 degrees. The name of the stroke is a bit confusing because the motion is a vertical swing, rather than the horizontal circular motion of a helicopter's blades.

Hip Clip – This refers to the trademark shot of cricketer Brian Lara. It involves a flicking wrist movement that whips a ball at a right angle past the fielder. It is so called because the ball is typically whipped at hip height.

Hit Wicket – This refers to a batsman getting dismissed as he attempts to take a run or play the ball, but ends up dislodging the bails with either his body or his bat. This is governed under the laws of cricket by Law 35. This is ranked sixth in the most common methods of dismissal in cricket.

Hoik – This term refers to an unrefined shot that's played to leg side, typically across the ball's line. The meaning of the term is similar to that of slog, but it's mostly used for shots that aren't in the cricket coaching book. Simply put, a hoik is a wild shot that's played without style.

Hold-up an End – This refers to the act of a batsman of deliberately restricting their team's scoring and focusing on defence while his batting partner does the scoring at his end. This term may also refer to bowlers who restrict runs at their own end. It is generally believed that all cricketers should learn how to hold-up an end.

Hole Out – This refers to getting dismissed as a result of being caught. This usually refers to a catch made after a lofted shot, as opposed to being caught by the wicket-keeper. Simply put, the term refers to a batsman hitting the ball to a fielder and being caught.

Hoodoo – When a bowler has gotten a batsman out several times in his career, it is said that he "has the hoodoo" on that batsman. the term was coined in reference to an ancient African-American folk magic, since the bowler seems to be using magic on the batsman, thus always getting him out.

Hook – This term refers to a shot that has similarities to a pull. The main difference is that this shot is played such that the cricket ball is struck as it reaches a point just above the shoulder of the batsman. This shot is also played particularly against a cricket ball that bounces above chest height, thus requiring the batsman to "hook" the ball.

Hot Spot – This is a technology commonly used in TV coverage for evaluating bat-pad catches and snicks. It is so called because an infrared camera is used in filming and the friction caused by the bat hitting the ball is seen as a white spot on the screen. This actually requires the use of two infrared cameras positioned on opposite sides of the field.

Howzat – This term refers to the call a fielding team makes when they appeal. It is notable because umpires aren't allowed to dismiss a batsman unless this question is asked. It is a derivative of the question, "How's that?"

Hutch – This term refers to the dressing room or pavilion, particularly one that's considered home to a significant number of rabbits.

-I-

In – This term refers to the state of the batsman who is presently batting. When a batsman is ready to bat, therefore, he is said to be In. This is in contrast to being dismissed or being Out.

Incoming Batsman – This refers to a batsman who is next in line to bat. When there's a Timed Out, the incoming batsman is the one being dismissed. The incoming batsman has to be ready to bat within three minutes once a batsman is out to avoid a Timed Out being called.

In-swing – This term refers to a ball delivery that curves in the air from off side to leg side and into the batsman. Such a delivery is typically executed by a swing bowler. It is also known as an in-swinger.

In-Cutter – This refers to a delivery which, after hitting the ground, goes into the batsman. This delivery is typically used by a medium pacer for the purpose of producing some late ball movement. This is usually executed after 10-15 overs, when the ball has lost its shine.

Infield – This refers to the area of the cricket field that lies within the 30-yard circle. Back when there were still no defined circles, this was the area near the wicket with an imaginary line running through cover point, mid-off, mid-on, and square leg. This area is the usual reference point for restrictions in fielding, particularly in short versions of the game.

Innings – This refers to a team's turn to either bat or bowl. This is a game segment with a fixed length. In cricket, the term "innings" can both be singular and plural.

-J, K-

Jaffa – This term refers to an exceptionally bowled delivery that's usually executed by a fast bowler. It is so called because a Jaffa is believed to be the best variety of orange. This is also sometimes called a Corker.

Jockstrap – This term refers to the underwear of male cricketers. This is designed specifically to secure a cricket box, particularly when the player is wicket-keeping or batting. This typically consists of a support pouch for the male genitalia and a waistband.

K

Keeper – This term is a shortened version of wicket-keeper. This player stands behind the stumps. He is the only player on the fielding team who is allowed to wear external leg guards and gloves.

King Pair – This is another term for a Golden Pair. It refers to an instance when the batsman gets dismissed off the very first ball he faced in both innings in a two-innings game. This means the batsman doesn't score any runs in any of the innings.

Knock – This term refers to the innings of a batsman. When a batsman scores high in an innings, he is said to have experienced a "good knock." In case a batsman makes 40 runs comprised of 5 fours and 4 sixers, he is said to have made a knock of 40 with 5 fours and 4 sixers.

Kolpak – This term refers to an overseas player participating in domestic cricket in England under Kolpak ruling. This ruling was handed down in 2003, favouring Slovak handball player Maros Kolpak. The ruling allowed citizens of countries with signed agreements with the EU to work and move within the EU in the same way EU citizens do.

Kookaburra – This refers to a cricket ball exclusively used in New Zealand, South Africa, and Australia, particularly in Test Cricket. All ODI matches use this ball, except for test matches played in India, which use SG cricket balls. Kookaburra balls have been in use since 1946.

Kwik Cricket – This term refers to an informal version of the game, which is designed specifically to introduce the sport to children. It is a high-speed game that encourages children to participate in the sport. Although most of the rules applied are taken from cricket, the game uses a plastic ball and bat.

-L-

Lappa – This is an Indian version of a hoik. The term is taken from the English word "lap." It refers to a stroke that's somewhere between a sweep and a pull. It also traces its origins to the Hindi word "lappet," which means "wind."

Leading Edge – This term refers to the cricket ball striking the bat's front edge rather than its face, particularly when the batsman is executing a cross-bat shot. This usually leads to an easy catch for a bowler. For someone else, it can result in a skier.

Leave – This refers to a batsman's act of not making any attempt to play the ball. This may be done by holding the cricket bat above the body. However, a batsman becomes more susceptible to being dismissed if he does this. This also prevents the batsman from claiming any leg byes.

Left Arm – This term refers to a bowler using his left hand to bowl. Such a bowler is traditionally called a left arm bowler rather than a left-handed bowler. In contrast, a batsman who holds the bat in his left hand is called a left hand batsman.

Left Hand – This term refers to a batsman who holds the bat in his left hand. This is in contrast to a left arm bowler, who is never called a left hand bowler. In cricket history, left hand batsmen are among the most stylish and productive players.

Left Stranded – This term refers to a batsman who fails to achieve a century as a result of running out of batting partners or having a successful run end. In this case, the batsman is denied a century even if his wicket hasn't been taken.

Leg before Wicket – This refers to a method of dismissing a batsman. If the umpire deems that the ball hit the batsman's body before it hit the bat, the batsman is dismissed. It is so called because it's usually the batsman's leg that gets hit before the ball strikes the bat and goes on to the wicket; hence, hitting the leg before the wicket.

Leg Break – This refers to a particular leg spin delivery that turns from the leg to the off side for right-handed players. In this case, the ball usually turns as the ball pitches. This delivery is also known as a wrist spinner.

Leg Bye – This refers to extras that are taken after a particular delivery hits the batsman's body other than his gloved hand or bat. This extra is not likely to be scored if the batsman doesn't attempt to execute a play. If a run is gained, it will be added to the team's total score, but not to the batsman's individual statistics.

Leg Cutter – This refers to a break delivery executed by either a medium-pace or fast bowler. The action is similar to that made by spin bowler, but the pace is faster. The ball in this case breaks from the batsman's leg to off side.

Leg Glance – This refers to a gentle shot executed at a ball that's aimed slightly towards the leg side. The shot is played by flicking the ball with the bat as it goes past the batsman, thus deflecting it towards the fine leg area. The bat is held vertically in this case.

Leg Side – This term refers to half of the cricket field that's at the batsman's rear as he takes a shot. This area is also called the on side. For a right hand batsman, this term refers to the left half of the cricket field.

Leg Slip – This term refers to a fielding position that's equivalent to the slip, but is at the leg side. This is a catching position that's designed specifically to catch the cricket ball after it deflects slightly from the bat's edge. The term is also used to refer to the fielder holding the position.

Leg Spin – This refers to a bowling style wherein the bowler imparts a spin on the cricket ball with a turn of the wrist as he delivers it. Because of this wrist movement, the style is also called a wrist spin. Only right arm bowlers who bowl this way are typically called leg spinners; left arm bowlers are typically called unorthodox spinners.

Leg Theory – This refers to a bowling attack style wherein cricket balls are aimed at the leg side. The aim of this style is to give the batsman limited room to execute a shot. This is generally considered as boring play by commentators and spectators because it results in very few runs scored.

Leggie – This is another term used to refer to a leg spinner. It is also used in reference to a leg break.

Length – This term refers to the area along the pitch wherein a delivery bounces. It is also defined as the distance a ball bounces down the pitch on its way towards the batsman. It is often described as being short, good, or full.

Life – This is a noun used to refer to a batsman who is reprieved due to the fielding team's mistake. The mistake leading to the reprieve could be a dropped catch, a missed run-out chance, or a missed stumping.

Light – This term is a short cut for bad light. When weather conditions make it too dark to bat safely, the umpire is likely to offer the batsmen an option to stop the play. A batsman may also appeal to the umpire if he deems it too dangerous to continue the play. These days, a light metre is used to determine if there's adequate light to continue play.

Limited Overs Match – This term refers to a single-innings match wherein each team is required to face only a particular number of overs. This is also known as one-day cricket. Important matches of this type typically set aside two days, with the second day being a reserve in case a result isn't reached on day one.

Line – This refers to a deviation of a point along a cricket pitch where a bowled ball typically bounces wicket-to-wicket from the line. The simplest definition of a line is the path a ball takes towards the batsman. Horizontally, it is the action of the ball running from off side to leg side.

Line and Length Bowling – This refers to the act of bowling such that the delivery pitches outside off stump with a good length. This style of bowling forces a batsman to execute a shot, since the ball could hit the stumps. In cricket, line and length are often discussed together.

List A Cricket – This term refers the equivalent of limited-overs in first-class cricket. Just as first-class cricket is a level below test cricket, List A cricket is also a level below One-day International. Most countries participating in the sport have a form of List A cricket.

Long Hop – This refers to a delivery that's too short to be called good length, but doesn't have the sharp lift characteristic of a bouncer. This is usually considered as bad delivery, since it gives the batsman plenty of time to plan and execute an attacking shot. The term has also become slang for an argument that can easily be refuted.

Long On – This term refers to a field position located near the boundary towards the leg side. The main responsibility of the position is sweeping up straight drives. The main goal is to prevent batsmen from scoring runs from on drives.

Loop – This term refers to the curved path taken by a ball that's delivered by a spinner. The term is also used to describe the flight of the ball after it is thrown or hit. It also refers to a bowling aspect.

Loosener – This term refers to a poor delivery that's bowled right at the beginning of the bowler's spell. This may result in a no ball, a wide ball, a beamer, a long hop, or a full toss. This usually occurs as a result of a lack of preparation coupled with a special focus on hitting the mark.

Lower Order – This refers to batsmen assigned at number 8-11 in the team's batting order. these batsmen may have batting skills, but generally specialise in bowling or wicket-keeping. Their batting ability is usually limited.

Luncheon – This term refers to the first interval taken during a day's play. This typically occurs during lunchtime; hence, its name. It is commonly shortened to lunch and usually lasts for 40 minutes.

-M-

Maiden Over – This refers to an over where there are no runs scored off the bat. At the same time, there are no no-balls or wides bowled. This is generally considered as a good performance by a bowler. It is tracked and recorded as part of bowling analysis.

Maker's Name – This refers to a cricket bat's full face where you would normally find the manufacturer's logo. It is particularly used in reference to a technique where a batsman plays a straight drive. A batsman who plays an especially good straight shot is said to have shown the maker's name to the ball.

Manhattan – This refers to a bar graph showing runs scored off every over in a single-day game. Dots are typically used to indicate overs wherein wicket fell. Also called a Skyline, the graph is so called because it is said to resemble Manhattan's skyline.

Mankad – This refers to a non-striking batsman running-out by leaving his crease while the bowler hasn't released the ball yet. This is quite common in indoor games, but almost never happens in first-class games. It takes its name from Indian bowler Vinoo Mankad, who used the tactic during a Test match.

Man of the Match – This term refers to an award that may be accorded to the batsman with the highest score, the player with the most wickets taken, or the best performer overall in a match. Although the award may be given to a member of either team, it is usually conferred to a member of the winning team. The actual award may be cash, a trophy, or champagne.

Marillier Shot – This refers to a shot executed with the bat parallel to the cricket pitch with the bat's toe pointed towards the bowler. This is an attempt by the batsman to flick the cricket ball above the wicket-keeper's head. This shot is also called Dilscoop and Paddle Scoop.

Marylebone Cricket Club – This is the owner of the Lord's cricket ground located in London NW8. The club serves as custodian for the laws of cricket. It was founded in 1787.

Match Fixing – This refers to the act of bribing a player or players of one team so they'll deliberately deliver a poor performance. The usual intention is to win bets on the game results. This practice is not only a violation of game rules, but also of the law.

Match Referee – This term refers to the game official who is responsible for ensuring the so-called spirit of the game is maintained at all times. He has the authority to fine teams and players for unethical play. He stays off the field and observes the game from a particular spectators' area.

Meat of the Bat – This term refers to the thickest portion of a cricket bat. It is from this part where the highest amount of energy is transferred to the ball. When a batsman hits the ball with this part of his bat, he is said to have connected really well. He is also said to have middle it.

Medium-pace – This refers to a bowler whose pace is faster than that of a spin bowler, but slower than that of a pace bowler. Although they try to defeat batsmen with ball movement rather than pace, speed is still important to this type of bowler. They either rely on the cricket ball swinging in the air or bowl cutters.

Michelle – This is another term used to refer to a five-wicket haul. This term is taken from the name of Michelle Pfeiffer, since a five-wicket haul is also known as a five-for or a fifer.

Middle of the Bat – This refers to the area of a bat's face that provides maximum power to the batsman's shot when it hits the ball. This is similar to the sweet spot, except that when you say a shot has been middle, it usually means the ball is hit with excellent timing and great power. This is also called meat of the bat.

Middle Order – This refers to a batsman who bats at number 5-7 in their team's batting order. These players are usually more comfortable with attacking strokes, but they usually don't have complete technique, which is necessary for batting for long periods. This batting order is usually comprised of wicket-keepers and all-rounders.

Mid-wicket – This term refers to a fielding position on the leg side that mirrors deep extra cover seen on the off side. This position is designed specifically to either prevent runs from an on drive or catch the cricket ball from misplaced pull shots. This is between the mid-on and the square leg.

Military Medium – This refers to medium-pace bowling which lacks the necessary speed to make the play difficult for a batsman. The term usually has a derogatory overtone, suggesting that the bowling is innocuous and boring. But, it may also be used to praise a bowler, suggesting military regularity and consistency.

Mine – This refers to the term yelled by a fieldsman when he calls a catch. In doing so, he announces to the other fieldsmen that he's in the right position to take a catch. This is generally considered good practice because it prevents a fieldsman from colliding with another fieldsman when they attempt to make the same catch.

Mis-field – This term refers to a fielder who fails to cleanly collect the cricket ball. Common examples are dropping a catch and fumbling a pickup. Simply put, it is the failure to correctly field a ball.

Mongoose Bat – This refers to a cricket bat that's designed specifically for Twenty20 cricket. It has an unusual design because the blade is typically 33% shorter than conventional bats, while the handle is typically 43% longer. This bat has been declared legal and may be used in any cricket game at any level.

Mullygrubber – This term refers to a cricket ball that fails to bounce after pitching. Legendary commentator and cricketer Richie Benaud was the one who coined the term. This tactic is generally considered as a sign that the bowler has run out of ideas and will use just about any method available to win the game.

-N-

Negative Bowling – This refers to the persistent bowling down the batsman's leg side to prevent him from scoring. This is often used in Test matches. The object is to frustrate the batsman and possibly cause him to make the wrong shots such that gets dismissed.

Nelson – This refers to a 111 score either by an individual or a team. This is considered as an unlucky score and batsmen are believed to be at risk of being dismissed at this point. To avert the bad luck, it is said that spectators need to stand on just one leg.

Nervous Nineties – This refers to a period within a batsman's innings where his score is at 90-99. At this point, players usually bat very cautiously to avoid getting dismissed before they achieve a century. It is so called due to the pressure felt by the batsman.

Nets – This term refers to a pitch that's surrounded by netting on three sides. This is used by bowlers and batsmen for practice. The purpose of the netting is to prevent the cricket ball from going too far.

Net Run Rate – This refers to the run rate of a winning team minus the run rate of the losing team. The positive value goes to the winning team and the negative value to the losing team. In a cricket series, the NRR mean is taken from all matches played by a team.

New Rock – This term refers to a new and unused cricket ball. The fielding team's captain typically takes a new ball at a certain time within an innings as replacement for the one currently being used. The term is also used in reference to the bowler bowling with the new cricket ball or the batsman who faces the new ball.

Nibble – This refers to an instance wherein a batsman makes an indecisive push at a delivery that pitched on the outside of off stump instead of just leaving it. This often leads to an edge to the slips or wicket-keeper. The term is taken from the tentative way a mouse nibbles at cheese.

Nick – This is another term for snick or edge. It refers to a small deflection made by the ball off the bat's edge. It may also be used as a verb in reference to the act of using the bat's edge to hit the ball, thus producing a fine deflection.

Nightwatchman – This refers to a particular lower order batsman who's sent in as the light grows dim. He usually plays in the game's remaining overs for the day so that more valuable batsmen are protected for the following day's play. His primary responsibility is to maintain the strike until the play closes.

No Ball – This term refers to an illegal delivery. In this case, the batting team is awarded an extra. The bowler will need to deliver another ball at which point the batsman may not be dismissed.

No Man's Land – This refers to an area within the pitch without any fielders near it. The term is normally used when the batsman mis-times his shot and is fortunate enough to have the ball land where no fielder can catch it.

Non-striker – In cricket, there are always two batsmen playing at any given time. This term refers to the batsman who stands at bowling end. In this case, it is his partner who has the responsibility of striking the ball.

Not Out – This refers to a batsman who hasn't been dismissed yet, particularly at the end of play. The term also refers to the umpire's call when he turns down the bowling team's appeal for a wicket. In the scorecards, the batsman's score is appended, usually with an asterisk, to show his Not Out status.

Nurdle – This refers to the act of scoring runs by nudging the ball gently into vacant parts of the cricket field. The act is also referred to as milking around. The aim of this move is to score a quick single.

Odds Match – This refers to a cricket match wherein one team has more players. The extra players are generally allowed to both bat and field. As a result, the bowling team may have over 11 fielders at a given time.

One Day International – This term refers to a cricket match played by two national teams. It is typically limited to fifty overs for each innings. It is so called because the match is played in just one day.

Off Break – This refers to the kind of off spin delivery where the ball turns from off to leg side for right arm bowlers and right hand batsmen. This is known as the off spin bowler's attacking delivery. It is also known as an off spinner.

Off Cutter – This refers to a kind of off break delivery that's typically bowled by either a medium-pace or fast bowler. In this case, the ball typically goes into the batsman right after it hits the ground. The turn of this delivery isn't as sharp as an off break, but it can still cause the batsman some difficulties due to the speed of delivery.

Off Side – This refers to the side of the pitch that's facing the batsman as he bats. For a right hand batsman, this refers to the right side of the cricket pitch. It is so called because it is the side away from the legs of the batsman.

Off Spin – This refers to a bowling style wherein the bowler uses his fingers to impart spin on the cricket ball as it is delivered. The move is therefore also called finger spin. It is typically the right arm bowlers who bowl this way who are called off spinners. Left arm bowlers are described as either orthodox or unorthodox.

Off the Mark – This term refers to the first run a batsman scores. A batsman who gets dismissed without scoring is said to have failed in getting off the mark. The first team to score in a match is said to be first off the mark.

On Side – This term refers to the half of a cricket pitch that's behind the batsman as he takes a shot. For a right hand batsman, this is the left half of the cricket pitch. It is also known as the leg side.

On a Length – This term describes a delivery that's executed on a good length. A good length is generally described as a ball which the batsman finds difficult to decide whether to play by going forward or back. The purpose of bowling such a delivery is to create doubt in the batsman's mind, which often leads to mistakes.

On Strike – This term refers to the batsman who is currently faced with the bowling attack. This batsman is said to have the state of being on strike, which is why he is called a striker.

On the Up – This term refers to a batsman, usually one who's playing a drive to a cricket ball that's a bit short. The ball in this case has typically risen to at least knee height as the batsman plays the shot. One of the most famous batsmen able to hit this kind of shot is West Indies cricketer Vivian Richards.

One-day Cricket – This refers to a shortened form of cricket, characterised by a single innings per team. It is so called because it's typically played in one day with limited overs. This is also known as limited overs cricket.

One Down – This refers to the batsman who is third on the batting order. This is considered as a crucial position, which is why the most technically proficient batsman is typically assigned to it. This batsman should aim for a significant number of runs.

One Short – This term refers to a batsman failing to ground his bat or himself beyond the popping crease before he turns to make an additional run. As a result, a run will be knocked off the batsman's score. If, however, a batsman deliberately runs short, no runs will be counted.

Opener – This term refers to a batsman who is especially skilled at batting right at the start of an innings, while the ball is still new. The aim of this batsman is to get their innings off to a positive start. It also refers to a bowler who opens the innings, usually a fast bowler.

Orthodox – This term refers to shots that are played in textbook manner. It is also used to refer to batsmen who play this way. More specifically, the term refers to left arm spin bowlers who use their fingers to spin the ball, thus imparting spin the same way a right arm spin bowler does.

Out – This term refers to the state of a dismissed batsman. There are generally ten ways to declare a batsman out. The term also refers to the word spoken by the umpire as he raises his index finger to answer an appeal for wicket affirmatively.

Out Dipper – This term refers to a dipper which, just before pitching, curves away rather than into the batsman. The direction of the ball in this case is from leg side to off side.

Outswing – This term refers to a delivery which curves in the direction away from the batsman. Bowlers who bowl this type of delivery are known as swing bowlers. This is often considered as a very difficult fast delivery for right hand batsmen to play.

Outfield – This refers to the area of a cricket field that lies outside the 30-yard circle that's measured from the middle of the pitch. Less formally, it is known as the area within the pitch that's farthest away from the wickets. This area is closest to the boundary.

Over – This term refers to a bowler's act of delivering six consecutive balls. In Australia, an over is traditionally the delivery of eight consecutive balls. At the end of one over, the fielding team is required to switch ends and the bowler is replaced.

Over Rate – This term refers to the total number of overs that was bowled per hour. There is a minimum over rate a fielding team needs to adhere to. If an international team does not reach the minimum twice in a 12-month period in the same game format, the team captain is suspended for a match.

Over the Wicket – This refers to a right arm bowler who bowls to the left side of the stumps or a left arm bowler bowling to the right side of the stumps. This puts the bowler's dominant hand nearer the wicket. This style of delivery is the opposite of around the wicket.

Overarm – This refers to the act of a bowler delivering the ball by letting his arm swing behind his body and then over his head. The ball is released as it approaches the downswing and the bowler's elbow remains straight. This is normally the only type of bowling allowed in cricket matches.

Overpitched Delivery – This refers to a delivery that's full pitched, although it doesn't qualify as a Yorker, as it bounces right in front of a batsman. This is considered as poor delivery because the batsman can easily hit the ball with the middle of the bat in this case. This often results in a half-volley.

Overthrows – This term refers to the feat of scoring extra runs as a result of a fielder's errant throw. The term is also used in reference to the throw itself. Another term for this feat is Buzzers.

-P-

Pace Bowling – This refers to a bowling style wherein the ball is delivered at speeds of over 90mph. For this reason, the style is also known as fast bowling. This is one of the main approaches to cricket bowling.

Pads – This term refers to protective equipment used by wicket-keepers and batsmen to cover their legs. They protect the players' legs from the impact caused by hard balls at high speed. They're also known as leg guards.

Pad Away – This refers to the act of using the pads to hit the ball such that it veers away from the wicket. This play is only possible if there's no danger of getting out LBW. Using the pad saves the batsman from being caught by the close fielders.

Paddle Sweep – This refers to an extremely fine sweep, appearing almost as a mere tickle of a delivery pitched on leg stump. This is a variation of the standard sweep shot. Rather than relying on the power of the shot, the paddle sweep relies on accurate ball placement.

Paddle Scoop – This refers to a shot wherein the ball is scooped over the batsman's shoulder. The aim is to find a boundary in the fine leg area or behind the wicket-keeper. This is a modern shot that's now being used quite often in Twenty20 and One Day International matches.

Pair – This is an abbreviated version of "pair of ducks" or "pair of spectacles." It refers to a score of zero runs earned by a batsman in both of his innings in a two-innings match. When a batsman gets out without scoring in an inning, the score is called a duck because the 0 figure resembles a duck's egg. Two zeros in two innings, therefore, constitute two ducks; hence, a pair.

Partnership – This refers to the total number of runs a batting pair scores before one batsman gets dismissed. Also included are the time taken and deliveries faced. Batsmen are always required to bat in partnership in the sport of cricket.

Part Time – This refers to a bowler who isn't expected to bowl at all times, but is good enough to bowl a few times. This bowler is often successful, since he presents some surprising attributes and offers variation in performance. This bowler is typically called on to bowl when the specialist bowlers aren't performing that well.

Pavilion – This term refers to the building complex or grandstand where the dressing rooms are located and members of the club who owns the ground are typically seated. Dressing rooms are generally found in the members' area. This is also where batsmen who are dismissed go.

Peach – This refers to a delivery from a fast bowler that's described as unplayable. This is generally considered as a very good delivery. In fact, it's typically so good that the batsman can't even edge and is often dismissed as a result.

Perfect Over – For a bowler, this term would refer to a maiden over. For a batsman, this would refer to scoring six sixes off the same bowler in one over. Consistency is perhaps the most important attribute for achieving the perfect over.

Perfume Ball – This refers to a bouncer outside off-stump passing within a few inches of a batsman's face. It is so called due to the fact that the ball is said to be close enough for the batsman to smell.

Picket Fences – This term refers to an over wherein a run is scored off every delivery. The scorecard in this case will show 111111, which looks like a picket fence; hence, the name.

Pie Chucker – This refers to a poor bowler whose deliveries are so flighted they appear like a pie up in the air. Such a delivery is very easy for a batsman to score off. The term was popularly used by batsman Kevin Pietersen in describing the delivery of Yuvraj Singh.

Pinch Hitter – This term refers to a batsman promoted from lower order to increase run rate. The batsman is given more freedom to play in this case, since less importance is placed on this wicket. The term is borrowed from the sport of baseball, although it doesn't quite mean the same thing.

Pitch – This refers to the rectangular area in the middle of a cricket field where a majority of the game's action takes place. Typically 22 yards long, this is usually made of clay or earth. This also refers to the action of a cricket ball bouncing before it reaches the batsman.

Pitch Up – This refers to the act of bowling on a fuller length. Full length deliveries bounce closer to a batsman than good length deliveries. This is opposite to banging it in.

Pitch Map – This term refers to a diagram that shows where balls delivered by a specific bowler have pitched. This diagram can help you understand a bowler's pitching areas. It is similar to a beehive.

Placement – This term refers to a ball hit in such a way that it either bisects or trisects fielders. This ball typically ends up as a four.

Platinum Duck – This term refers to the experience of a batsman being dismissed without facing a single ball. This usually happens when the non-striker is run out. This is also sometimes called a Diamond Duck.

Playing On – This refers to a batsman hitting the ball, but only succeeding in diverting it towards the stumps. As a result, the batsman is out bowled. This is also called chopping on or dragging on.

Plumb – This term refers to an obvious and indisputable dismissal, such as LBW. When this happens, the batsman is said to be plumb LBW or obviously LBW. As regards a wicket, it refers to giving true bounce.

Point – This term refers to a fielding position that's square of the off side of the batsman. This position is between the cover and the gully. The term is also used in reference to the fielder holding the position.

Point of Release – This term refers to the bowler's position as he releases the ball. It is part of the bowling action. It differs according to the type of delivery bowled.

Pongo – This term is used to describe an extremely high volume of batting assault or run-making. The term is primarily used by UK county cricketers.

Popper – This term refers to a ball rising sharply from the cricket pitch when bowled. It is so called because the ball's movement makes it appear to pop up.

Popping Crease – This refers to a line on the field that's four feet parallel to and in front of the bowling crease where wickets are positioned. This line borders unsafe and safe territory for a batsman as he takes runs. When a batsman reaches this crease without any part of his bat or body touching the ground, he is in danger of getting dismissed.

Powerplay – This refers to a certain block of overs, which offer temporary advantage for the batting team in One Day Internationals. It also refers to the specific number of overs with fielding restrictions in a One Day International match. This rule was introduced to make the game more interesting and competitive.

Pro20 – This term refers to the South African version of Twenty20. The T20 was originally introduced in Wales and England in 2003. In this match, each team is required to play only one innings and bat for only as much as 20 overs.

Pro40 – This is the name given to a limited overs match played in England during the late summer. In this case, games involve group stages and later knockout stages for qualifiers. It is so called because there are typically 40 over for each side.

Projapoti – This refers to a zero rotation variation ball. When bowled correctly, the ball moves in an erratic manner in flight, similar to a butterfly. The term was coined by fielding coach Julien Fountain and bowling coach Ian Pont of Bangladesh. Projapoti is the Bengali word for butterfly.

Protected Area – This refers to an area of the cricket pitch that's defined as starting five feet from the popping crease with a width of two feet down the centre of the pitch. Bowlers are prohibited from trespassing the area in his follow-through. A warning is given for doing so and if he receives three warnings of this sort, he will be barred from bowling further in the innings.

Pull – This refers to a shot that's played to a short-pitched delivery on the leg side. The shot is played between backward square-leg and mid-wicket. This is typically played at waist height with the arms extended.

Pursuit – This term is synonymous with run chase. During the fourth innings of a Test or first-class match, there's a set number of runs that needs to be attained to achieve victory. This is referred to as a pursuit or run chase.

-Q, R-

Queen Pair – This refers to a batsman who is out without scoring any runs off of the second ball faced in both innings during a two-innings match. This isn't a traditional cricketing term, but it has been used often enough that you're likely to encounter it in many cricket commentary.

Quick – Traditionally, this term referred to a bowler who completes his over very quickly. In recent years, the term has been used synonymously with a pace bowler or fast bowler. The irony is that quick bowlers traditionally bowled slow deliveries.

Quota – This refers to the total amount of overs allotted to one bowler in a limited overs or ODI match. This is typically calculated as total overs in an innings divided by five and then rounded off to the next higher integer.

R

Rabbit – This term refers to a specialist bowler who's particularly bad at batting. He is often seen as being unsure even of how the bat should be held. The term may also refer to a batsman who frequently gets out to the same bowler.

Rain Rule – This refers to any one of the various methods to determine the winner of a one-day match shortened by rain. The currently preferred method for doing so is the Duckworth-Lewis method. There are more than ten other rain rule methods to choose from.

Red Cherry – This term is a nickname given to the cricket ball. It is attributed to the cherry red colour of the ball. Sometimes it is shortened to cherry.

Referral – This refers to a system allowing fielding captains and batsmen to appeal to the third umpire as regards a particular decision. This is still in an experimental stage and as such isn't used for Test matches yet. Those who support the system claim it should be made permanent because it's the closest to a perfect system cricket is ever going to get.

Required Run Rate – This is the same as the asking rate. It is typically calculated by dividing the number of runs required to win the game by the number of balls remaining. For example, if there are eight overs left and the required run is 32, then the required run rate is 32/8 or 4.

Reserve Day – This refers to a free day in the schedule of a touring team. This day may be used to reconvene or replay a match that's washed out. This usually occurs in the late stages of limited-overs tournaments.

Rest Day – This refers to a day when there's no game in a multiple-day match. These were common in the earlier days of cricket, but are now seldom seen. It does still happen occasionally in Test matches.

Retire – This refers to the batsman's act of voluntarily leaving the field, usually due to injury. A player retiring due to injury may still return when a wicket falls in the innings. However, a player who retires without injury may return only if the opposing team's captain agrees.

Reverse Sweep – This refers to a right hand batsman sweeping like a left hand batsman and vice-versa. This is played by kneeling with the knee of the back leg on the pitch. The batsman then swings the bat horizontally from leg to off side.

Reverse Swing – This refers to the act of swinging the cricket ball in a manner contrary to conventional swinging. This is usually delivered with an older ball, but bowler skill and atmospheric conditions are also important factors. This was invented by Pakistani bowler Sarfaraz Nawaz.

Rib Tickler – This refers to a ball that's bowled short of length. As a result, the ball bounces higher than expected, striking the batsman in his midriff and hitting several ribs. Needless to say, this isn't an ideal ball to play.

Right Arm – This refers to a right-handed bowler. The term "right-handed" is rarely used in cricket to describe a bowler. In contrast, a batsman is typically described as right hand or left hand as opposed to right arm or left arm.

Right Hand – This refers to a right-handed batsman. The terms "right hand" and "left hand" are typically used to describe batsmen in cricket, but never bowlers. A right hand batsman typically faces south.

Ring Field – This refers to a field set mainly to save singles. It consists of fieldsmen in most or all primary positions towards the front of the wicket, within the area where the fielding circle would be. The positions occupied in this case are point, cover, mid off, mid on, midwicket, and square leg.

Road – This term refers to a very flat and hard pitch. This kind of pitch is considered very good for batting.

Rogers – This refers to the second team of a county or cricket club. The term was coined from the name of New Zealand cricketer Roger Twose. The career ODI average of Twose is the highest recorded by any New Zealand batsman.

Roller – This refers to a cylindrical tool that's used for flattening the pitch prior to play. It generally takes 8-10 hours to roll the field during the pre-season. To roll a wicket, the usual time required is 12-16 hours.

Rotate the Strike – This refers to the act of trying to make singles in every possible way. The aim is to make sure both batsmen continue making runs and facing deliveries. This is in direct contrast to farming the strike.

Rough – This refers to a worn-down part of the pitch. The wear and tear is often the result of bowlers' footmarks. Spinners take advantage of this area by obtaining more turn.

Roundarm Bowling – This refers to bowling action where the outstretched hand of the bowler lies perpendicular to his body as the ball is released. This was originally introduced in the 19th century. Over the years, this style was replaced by overarm bowling.

Run Chase – This refers to the act of the second batting team, particularly in a limited-overs game, trying to win by surpassing the accumulated runs of the opposing team. This also refers to a match situation where the last team to bat needs to reach a certain score in order to win, particularly if the remaining time makes it difficult to reach the target. Additionally, the term is used in reference to the effort that's made by the last team to bat.

Run Out – This refers to the dismissal resulting from a fielding team member breaking the wicket as the batsman is making a run outside his crease. To avoid getting run out, the batsman has to make contact with either his bat or his body with the ground inside the crease. This is just one of the various ways to dismiss a batsman.

Run Rate – This refers to the average number of runs that are scored in each over. This is calculated by dividing the number of runs with the number of overs it took to score them. This includes all of the runs, even the extras awarded as a result of bowling error.

Run Up – This refers to the act of running or walking to the bowling crease as part of the bowling process. It also refers to the area behind the pitch that a bowler uses for the run up. Every bowler has a different way of approaching the wicket, so there's a variety of run-ups.

Runner – This term refers to a player on the batting team who assists an injured batsman when running between wickets. In this case, the assisting runner must carry and wear the same equipment. He can also be run out along with the injured batsman.

-S-

Sawn Off – This term refers to a batsman wrongly given out. A number of teams have lost matches due to players being sawn off.

Scorer – This refers to the person recording the scores in the course of a game. He is responsible for recording all runs scored, wickets taken, and overs bowled. Two scorers are typically appointed in professional games.

Seam – This term refers to the stitching typically seen on the equator of a cricket ball. This also refers to the ball's sideways movement as it moves towards the batsman. The term is also used in reference to a bowler who moves the ball using seam.

Seam Bowling – This refers to a style of bowling that takes advantage of the ball's uneven conditions. The aim is to make the ball deviate as it bounces off the pitch. This is in direct contrast to swing bowling.

Selector – This refers to a person assigned the task of selecting players for a team. The term is typically used in reference to choosing players for provincial, national, and other teams at professional cricket levels. A panel of selectors typically acts under the relevant administrative body's authority.

Session – This refers to the period of play from the start to lunch, from lunch to tea, and from tea to stumps. During these periods, players aren't allowed to leave the field, except when there's a change of innings. In Test matches, there are generally three sessions, namely: pre-lunch, post-lunch, and post tea.

Shepherd the Strike – This is the same as farming the strike. It refers to a batsman protecting a weaker batsman by deliberately receiving most of the balls bowled. This is done by either scoring runs or declining to score runs to achieve the desired result.

Shooter – This refers to a form of delivery where the ball skids after pitching. This is usually bowled at a quick pace and is difficult for a batsman to hit cleanly. In this case, the drift is just as important as the speed of the ball.

Short-pitched – This refers to a delivery where the ball bounces close to the bowler. The aim is to let the ball bounce above waist height. This is also known as a bouncer. In case the ball bounces low, it's known as long hop.

Shot – This refers to a batsman's act of hitting the ball with the bat. Shots are classified as orthodox and unorthodox. When a batsman hits or attempts to hit the ball, he is said to have played a shot.

Side On – This refers to a type of bowler who has his chest, hips, and back foot aligned and faced towards the batsman as he makes back foot contact. The term is also used in reference to a batsman with his shoulders and hips faced 90 degrees to the bowler.

Sightscreen – This refers to a large board typically placed behind a bowler and beyond the boundary. It is used to give contrast to the cricket ball and help the striker see the ball clearly when it's delivered. This is usually coloured white in contrast to a red ball or black in contrast to a white ball.

Silly – This refers to a modifier to some fielding positions' names. It denotes that they're unusually near the batsman. The most common examples are silly point, silly midwicket, silly mid-on, and silly mid-off.

Silly Nanny – This refers to a streak of poor bowls that usually results in substitution. When this happens, the crowd is likely to give out a chorus of dismay. In general, silly nannies are also known as persons who have a false sense of athleticism.

Single – This term refers to a run that's scored by batsmen running only once between the wickets. It is also defined as one run that's scored off one ball. For the score to be awarded, the batsmen need to run to the opposite crease while avoiding getting run out.

Sitter – This term refers to an easy catch that generally needs to be taken. In fact, this catch is so easy it's also described as undroppable. If a fielder manages to drop such a catch, the scene is likely to be repeatedly played on the replay screen, thus causing considerable embarrassment.

Six – This refers to a shot that touches or passes over the boundary without rolling or bouncing. It is so called due to the fact that it allows the batting team to score six runs. It is also known as a sixer.

Skier – This refers to a mistimed shot that's hit almost perfectly straight up into the air towards the sky. This usually results in a batsman getting caught out. There are times, however, when the fielder somehow misses or drops the catch, which is typically considered very embarrassing.

Skipper – This term is used in the same way as Captain. It can also be used as a verb to describe the act of taking the responsibility of a team captain. As team captain, this player has responsibilities and roles over and above that of regular players.

Skyline – This is another term for Manhattan. This is a bar graph drawn with runs on its Y axis and overs on its X axis. It is so called because the bars are said to resemble the Manhattan skyline.

Slash – This refers to a cut that's played aggressively or maybe even recklessly. A cut is normally played to a short-pitched delivery square on the off side. It is so called due to the cutting motion a batsman makes when he executes the shot.

Sledging – This refers to verbal abuse or a psychological tactic used in cricket. This is often used to break the concentration of players on the opposing team. Although it is quite common in the sport, it is generally considered as going against the true spirit of the game.

Slice – This term refers to a cut shot that's played with the cricket bat at an obtuse angle to the batsman. It also refers to the act of hitting the ball such that the bat's face draws across the ball's face to deflect it. It is so called because of the slicing motion made with the bat.

Slider – This refers to a delivery by a wrist spinner where backspin is imparted on the ball. This makes the ball travel a greater distance, but with a lower bounce. Leg break action is often used in this delivery.

Slip – This refers to a fielder close behind the batsman, off side right beside the wicket-keeper. A fast bowler may have a maximum of four slips. The term is also used to refer to the position occupied by the fielders themselves.

Slipper – This term refers to a player specialising in slips fielding. For example, "This player is a distinctly good slipper." The player may also be skilled in other positions, but the slips is where he works best.

Slog – This refers to a powerful shot that's usually hit into the air in the batsmen's attempt to achieve a six. This is often executed without much concern for using proper technique. This is typically played aggressively and with a quickly-swung bat.

Slog Overs – This refers to the last ten overs in an ODI match. This is usually when batsmen play most aggressively, thus scoring at extremely high rates.

Slog Sweep – This refers to a sweep shot that's hit hard into the air and over the boundary that's the same as for a hook. This is a form of slog exclusively used against spin bowlers. It is played by kneeling, with the knee of the back leg on the pitch, swinging the bat horizontally across the body.

Slogger – This term refers to a batsman who manages to hit plenty of slogs. It also refers to batsmen who constantly aim to score runs on just about every delivery. This kind of batsman is known for having high strike rates.

Slower Ball – This refers to a medium-pace delivery that's delivered by a fast bowler. This is designed specifically to trick the batsman into playing a shot too early and ending up skying the ball to a fielder. This tactic can have several variations.

Slow Left Armer – This term refers to an orthodox left arm finger spin bowler. This type of bowler is the left-arm equivalent of the off spinner. Among the most popular slow left armers are Daniel Vettori and Monty Panesar.

Snick – This refers to a slight deviation made by the cricket ball off the bat's edge. It can come off any of the four edges: inside, outside, top, or bottom. This is also known as an edge.

Snickometer – This refers to a device used for measuring the sound generated by a snick. This sound is generally shown on the device as a spike similar to the spike shown by a seismograph when an earthquake occurs. This is sometimes called a snicko.

Specialist – This refers to a player specifically selected for a particular skill. Such a player may be described as a specialist batsman, specialist bowler, or specialist wicket-keeper. This type of player is the opposite of an all-rounder.

Spectacles – This term means the same thing as pair. Two ducks appear as 0-0 on a scorecard, resembling a pair of spectacles. When there are two first ball ducks in a single match, it is usually called golden spectacles.

Spell – This refers to the total number of continuous overs that a bowler bowls prior to being relieved. This can also refer to the number of overs bowled by a single bowler in one innings. The term may also be used to refer to the act of relieving a bowler so he can rest.

Spider Graph – This refers to a graphical chart representing the cricket ball's trajectory from a scoring stroke. The graph shows the ball's direction, the distance it travelled, its elevation, and how it bounces. A coloured line represents each scoring stroke.

Spin Bowling – This refers to a bowling style wherein a spin bowler tries to trick the batsman by using his fingers or wrist to impart spin on the cricket ball. It's difficult for a batsman to hit the ball in this case because it's likely to deviate after bouncing. This is most effective if the ball travels slowly, which is why most spinners keep their pace at 40-55mph.

Splice – This refers to the joint between a bat's handle and blade. This is considered as the bat's weakest part. In case the ball hits this part, it will most probably dolly up, resulting in an easy catch.

Square – This refers to a field position that's perpendicular to the pitch and opposite of fine. It is also the area where cricket pitches are prepared. The term also refers to an imaginary line that extends the crease to the leg side boundary.

Square-cut – This refers to a cut shot that's played perpendicular to a delivery. This shot is said to be played square. This is hit almost 90 degrees from the wicket.

Stance – This refers to a batsman's posture as he holds his bat and faces a delivery. This is also known as the batting stance. The most important thing about a stance is proper balance.

Stand – This term is synonymous to partnership. A batting partnership is often described with the characteristic of being for a specific wicket. For example, a partnership for the third wicket is often called a third wicket stand. The term may also refer to an umpire officiating a match, as he is said to be standing in the match.

Standing Up – This refers to the position adopted by the wicket-keeper when a slow bowler is delivering. This position is typically near the stumps. The objective is to catch the ball and possibly stump the batsmen out.

Start – This refers to a batsman's situation of successfully avoiding getting dismissed for a few runs. In Australia, the term is generally taken to mean scoring twenty runs. Batting is generally a lot easier for a batsman after surviving this period, since he is likely to have settled into a good rhythm by that time.

Steaming In – This term refers to a bowler who takes a quick run-up to bowl. In this case, the bowler is referred to as steaming in to bowl.

Sticky Dog – This refers to a drying wicket that's very difficult to bat on. This was pretty common in the early days of the sport. In recent years, however, the act of routinely covering the pitches has made this quite uncommon.

Sticky Wicket – This term refers to a difficult and wet pitch usually resulting from rain. The term is also used to refer to any pitch that behaves unpredictably. Just like a sticky dog, this was more common during the early years when pitches weren't routinely covered.

Stock Bowler – This refers to a bowler with the responsibility of restricting the opposing team's scoring rather than taking wickets. This type of bowler is typically tasked to bowl several overs at a poor run rate to allow strike bowlers to rest or take wickets from the opposite end. The role of this bowler is the opposite of a strike bowler's role.

Stock Delivery – This term refers to the standard delivery of a bowler or the delivery most frequently bowled by a bowler. A bowler will usually have a stock delivery as well as one or more variations. This is also known as stock ball.

Stodgier – This term refers to a batsman who focuses on defending and scores only at mediocre rate. This is commonly subject to derogatory comments. However, it may also earn compliments because of the resilience and technique it showcases.

Stonewaller – This term refers to a batsman who focuses on playing defensively rather than making an attempt to score. In cricket history, stonewallers are said to have bored spectators to death because of their batting style. Perhaps the most popular stonewaller in the history of the sport is Geoffrey Boycott

Straight Bat – This term refers to a cricket bat held vertically or swung in a vertical arc. The term may be used as a noun as described above or as an adjective as in: "The batsman executed a straight bat shot." This shot can be played on both front and back feet.

Straight Up-and-Down – This is a pejorative term that describes a medium-paced or fast bowler who doesn't have the necessary skills to seam or swing the ball. It is so called because the ball doesn't spin in this case and the seam is positioned straight up and down.

Strangler – This refers to a dismissal where a batsman tries to execute a glance and ends up getting an inside edge instead, which is then caught by the wicket-keeper. It takes a great deal of skill to execute a very fine glance properly because of the risk it involves.

Street – This refers to a cricket pitch that batsmen find easy and bowlers find difficult to play on. This is sometimes also called highway, road, and several other synonyms.

Strike – This refers to the position of the batsman who actually faces delivery. This is the opposite of a non-striker. Keeping the strike means arranging runs on an over's last ball so as to bat on the first ball of the next over.

Strike Bowler – This refers to an attacking bowler who focuses on taking wickets rather than restricting the opposing team's scoring. This is usually an attacking spinner or a fast bowler bowling in short spells. His ability to take wickets is the primary reason for this bowler to be included in a team.

Strike Rate – This refers to a percentage that's equal to the total number of runs a batsman scores divided by the total number of balls he faced. A higher rate in this case indicates the batsman is very efficient. This can also refer to the average amount of deliveries a bowler bowls before he rakes a wicket. A lower rate in this case indicates a very efficient bowler.

Striker – This term refers to the batsman facing the deliveries. It's his responsibility to play shots so they can score runs. Such a batsman is said to be on strike.

Stroke – This refers to an attempt made by a batsman to make a shot or play at a particular delivery. This is actually a synonym of the term "shot." When used as a verb, it means to hit the cricket ball.

Stump – This refers to one of the vertical posts that comprise the wicket. It is also one of the ways to dismiss a batsman. The term could also refer to the end of the day's play.

Sun Ball – This refers to a bowling method wherein the ball is deliberately bowled at a sluggish pace and with great height. The aim is to distract the batsman's vision with the sun's rays. This often causes disastrous consequences.

Sundry – This term refers to a run that isn't attributed to a particular batsman. Examples of this are wides, no-balls, and byes. This is also known as an extra.

Supersub – Under One Day International cricket rules that were introduced in 2005, a team can have a twelfth man who may act as substitute. The substitute may replace any player and take over his bowling and batting duties. When the twelfth man substitutes for a player in this manner, he is known as a supersub. This rule was experimental and was cancelled in 2006.

Surrey Cut – This refers to an inside edge that often results from a drive narrowly missing the stumps. In this case, the ball will usually run to fine leg. This is also known as Harrow Drive, French Cut, or Chinese Cut.

Sweep – This refers to a shot that's played to a slow good length delivery. This is executed by going down on one knee and sweeping the ball to leg side. This is generally played to spinners wherein the bat is held low and horizontal.

Sweet Spot – This refers to the area on the cricket bat's face that provides maximum power with minimum effort when you hit the ball with it. This is also known as the meat or middle of the bat. Striking the ball with this spot is often called being well timed.

Swing – This refers to a bowling style that's usually delivered by medium-pace and fast bowlers. The fielding team normally polishes the ball only on one side such that as an innings continues, it will appear shiny on one side and worn on the other. If the bowler delivers the ball with its seam upright, air will normally travel faster on the shiny side, thus making the ball swing in the air.

Switch Hit – This refers to a shot the batsman plays by reversing both his grip and his stance. A right hand batsman will therefore play the shot as a left hand batsman in this case. This has prompted a lot of discussion about the impact it has on the rules of the game.

-T-

Tail – This refers to the last group of batsmen in a cricket team's batting order. This group is typically comprised of specialist bowlers who may be skilled at batting. The group usually has one or more rabbits. It is also known as the lower order.

Tail-ender – This refers to the batsman batting towards the very end of their team's batting order. This is usually a wicket-keeper or specialist bowler who is relatively poor in batting. The very last of the tail-enders are also called bunnies.

Target – This refers to the score the second batting team needs to attain in order to win the game. This is typically one run more than the score of the first team to bat. It becomes especially important to reach the target during the final innings of the game.

Tea – This term refers to the second interval in a day's play, which is generally called the tea interval because it is timed right about tea-time. In a match that lasts only one afternoon, this interval is typically taken between innings. This interval usually lasts for twenty minutes.

Tea Towel Explanation – This term refers to the popular comic explanation given for the laws of cricket. It is so called because the "explanation" was originally printed on tea towels by an enterprising individual back in the 1970s. Although it's quite difficult for someone who isn't very familiar with the sport to understand, this comic explanation does indeed get the gist of the game.

Teesra – This refers to a variation delivery bowled by off spin bowlers. The term is an Urdu word that means the third one. This delivery is also defined as a doosra that has extra bounce. The actual definition is yet to be definitively announced.

Test Match – This refers to a cricket game played over five days. It is comprised of unlimited overs and played between senior international teams only. This is considered as the highest level of cricket.

Textbook Shot – This refers to a shot that's played with perfect technique. It is also known as cricket shot. It is so called because these shots are typically found in plenty of coaching manuals.

Third Man – This refers to the position behind an off side wicket-keeper. This position is beyond the gully and slip areas. It is designed to prevent batsmen from making runs from edges.

Third Umpire – This refers to the off-field umpire who is equipped with a monitor. His assistance is usually sought by the on-field umpires whenever they're in doubt. Using the TV replays, he declares the final decision in such cases.

Through the Gate – This refers to a batsman being dismissed as a result of the ball passing between the pads and the bat prior to hitting the wicket. The player is said to have been bowled through the gate in this case. This is a variation of being clean bowled.

Throwing – This term refers to a bowling action wherein the bowler's arm is straightened as he makes the delivery. This is considered an illegal action. Used as a verb, it means to violate the prohibition on straightening the bowling arm while executing a delivery.

Tice – This is an old term used in reference to a Yorker. It is a ball that's bowled such that it strikes the ground a bat's length in front of a wicket.

Tickle – This refers to an edge played to the slips or the wicket-keeper. It can also refer to a gentle shot played to fine leg or third man. The term may also refer to the gentle touch of the ball against the bat.

Tie – This refers to an extremely rare result wherein the two competing teams have equal scores at the end of the game. In a Test match, a tie occurs when all innings are completed and the scores are the same. In a limited overs match, a tie occurs when the pre-determined number of overs has been bowled and the scores are the same. This should not be confused with a draw, wherein the scores aren't equal.

Tied Down – This refers to batsmen getting their run-making significantly restricted by the bowling team. This indicates a good performance by the bowlers and fielders of the bowling team. At the same time, it indicates mediocre or poor performance by the batsmen of the batting team.

Timed Match – This refers to a match with the duration based on a specific amount of time instead of a pre-determined number of overs. These matches usually end in a draw. First-class cricket often consists of such matches.

Timing – This refers to the art of hitting the ball such that it hits the sweet spot of the bat. Although it appears effortless, such a shot provides great speed to the cricket ball. It is generally believed that successful batting in cricket is mostly about timing rather than power.

Ton – This term refers to a hundred runs scored by just one batsman in one innings. This is more popularly known as a century. A batsman achieves this, he is said to have completed a ton.

Top Order – This refers to batsmen belonging to the top four in their team's batting order. This group is typically comprised of the team's most skilled batsmen. These batsmen are generally equipped with just the right temperament and technique to handle long periods of batting.

Top Spin – This refers to a forward rotation of the cricket ball. Such a rotation causes the ball to increase speed right after pitching. This is also known as being halfway between a bowler's stock delivery and the wrong 'un.

Tour – This refers to an organised series of matches that requires playing away from a team's home base. The term is commonly used in international cricket in reference to a team playing matches in another country. The team on tour will usually be required to play a number of matches against local teams.

Tourist – This term refers to a cricketer belonging to a touring team. Tourists usually play a Test match and a One Day International.

Track – This is another term for a cricket pitch. This is the area in the middle of the field between the wickets. The surface of a pitch is normally very flat and covered with short grass.

Trundler – This refers to a reliable and steady medium-pace bowler. This bowler may not be especially good, but neither is he especially bad. The term also refers to a slow bowler who may think that he's quick.

Twelfth Man – Traditionally, this would refer to the team's first substitute player sent in when a fielder is injured. In a Test match, each team names twelve players before the match and then reduces this to eleven right before play commences. This allows a bit of flexibility to the team captain in making his selection, depending on current conditions.

Twenty20 – This refers to a new and fast-paced form of the game. This type of game has a maximum limit of twenty overs for every innings; hence, the name. There are also other rule changes that were made to make the game more appealing.

-U,V,W-

Umpire – This term refers to the three official tasked to enforce the laws of the game. They are also known as the adjudicators of play. They make the decisions as regards runs scored, dismissals, and other aspects of the game. the umpire also presides over appeals and declares an over complete.

Umpire Decision Review System – This refers to a system that allows batsmen and the fielding captain to request a review of an umpire's decision. In this case, the third umpire will conduct the review using technological tools. As a result of the review, a dismissal may be awarded or overturned.

Underarm – This refers to the act of bowling wherein the arm swings from behind the bowler's body and follows a downswing arc. The ball is then released on the upswing with the elbow remaining straight. This is now considered as an illegal bowling style in formal cricket.

Under-spin – This term refers to the backward rotation of the cricket ball, which causes it to reduce speed right after pitching. This is also known as a back-spin. This type of spin makes the ball drop slower and travel farther than it would in a normal delivery.

Unorthodox – This refers to a shot that's played in a manner other than the textbook manner. The term is also used to refer to a left arm bowler who uses his wrist to spin the ball. So called because it imparts spin the same way a right arm off spin bowler would.

Unplayable Delivery – This refers to a ball that's quite impossible for a batsman to handle successfully. The term is often used to indicate that the batsman got dismissed more because of the bowler's skill than due to his own error.

Upper Cut – This term refers to a shot typically played against a bouncer or short ball. In this case, the batsman executes a cut above his head, usually resulting in the ball going to the third-man area. This is also defined as a cut shot that usually sends the ball over the head of the wicket-keeper.

Uppish – This term describes a shot that gains quite a dangerous amount of height. This increases the possibility of a batsman being caught. When a batsman hits a ball this way, he is said to have hit it in an uppish manner.

V

Vee – This refers to an unmarked and loosely defined area on the cricket field on which the batsman stands. The two sides of this V-shaped area go throughthe mid-on and mid-off regions. The term also refers to the joint between the cricket bat's blade and the lower end of its handle.

Village – This refers to a cricket level that's played by a majority of cricket enthusiasts. The term was also traditionally used pejoratively when, in a professional match, the standard of play is unusually low. It is also known as village cricket.

W

Waft – This term refers to a loose and non-committal shot. This is typically played to a ball that's pitched wide of the off-stump and short of length. Furthermore, this shot is usually played with a casual approach.

Wag – This term refers to a situation wherein tail-enders manage to score more runs than they're expected to. This is considered among the most demoralising situations for a fielding team. The more runs the tail-enders score, the more demoralised the fielding team can become.

Wagon Wheel – This refers to a graphical chart that divides the cricket field into six sectors. It shows the number of runs a batsman scores in each area. The term may also be used in reference to a spider graph.

Walk – This refers to a batsman's act of walking off the pitch. He does so believing or knowing that he's out instead of waiting for the umpire to dismiss him. Although this has become increasingly rare, it's still considered as sporting behaviour.

Walking Wicket – This refers to an extremely poor batsman who is usually a specialist bowler. Statistically, the term is used to refer to a batsman averaging below 5. This is also sometimes used to refer to a normally good batsman who's in unusually poor form.

Wash Out – This may refer to a cricket match or a particular day in a match that's abandoned either with little play or no play because of rain. In many cases where a match is washed out, the match ends in a draw.

Wearing Wicket – This refers to the state of the pitch becoming worn in the course of play. When this happens, balls that land on the worn areas will turn more drastically, thus giving assistance to spin bowlers. This can also result in an uneven bounce.

Wicket – This term refers to a set of bails and stumps. It can also be used to refer to the pitch. Additionally, the term may be used in reference to a batsman's dismissal.

Wicket-keeper – This term refers to the player belonging to the fielding team who is positioned just behind the wicket on the batting end of the field. This player wears fielding gloves and should always be prepared to catch the ball in case the batsman misses it. This is a specialist position that's used for the entire duration of the game.

Wicket-keeper/batsman – This term refers to a wicket-keeper who's also very skilled in batting. This player is capable of playing in the opener position or at least scoring well in the top order.

Wicket Maiden – This refers to a maiden over wherein the bowler dismisses a batsman by taking a wicket. If two wickets were taken, then it's called a double wicket maiden. The batsman typically scores no runs in this case.

Wicket-to-wicket – This term refers to the imaginary line that connects the two wickets. This may also refer to a bowling style that's straight and unvaried.

Wide – This refers to a delivery passing illegally wide of the wicket. This typically results in an extra awarded to the batting team. The bowler is required to bowl an extra ball for each wide.

Without Troubling the Scorers – This term is synonymous to Duck. It refers to a batsman's score of zero. It is so called because the 0 on the scorecard resembled a duck's egg.

Wood – This refers to a bowler who's very consistent in dismissing a particular batsman while avoiding being substantially scored off. This bowler is said to have the wood over the batsman.

Worm – This term refers to a plot of a team's progressive run rate or their cumulative runs scored against the number of overs in a limited-overs match. It is so called because the graphical representation resembles a worm's wiggly path.

Wrong Foot – This refers to a situation where the bowler's front foot is used as his bowling foot. This action is known as bowling off the wrong foot. Consequently, a bowler who bowls in this manner is said to bowl off the wring foot.

Wrong Footed – This refers to a batsman's act of initially moving forward to or back from a delivery, but then suddenly changes the foot he uses. In this case, the batsman is described as having been wrong-footed. This usually applies to spin bowling.

Wrong 'Un – This term is another name for googly. The term is most commonly used in Australia. It refers to the kind of delivery where the ball turns in the opposite direction of the direction the batsman expected.

-X,Y,Z-

Xavier Tras – This term is slang for the number of extras awarded in an innings. The term is included on the scorecard as a hypothetical name for the batsman scoring the extras. It is often shortened to X. Tras.

Y

Yips – Bowlers occasionally experience the Yips when they lose confidence for some reason. This is a psychological condition wherein he is unable to relax when he delivers. This often results in the bowler holding the ball for too long before releasing it, thus making it lose flight, accuracy, and turn.

Yorker – This refers to a delivery pitched very near the batsman. The aim of this delivery is for the ball to pitch right under the batsman's bat. A perfectly executed Yorker is quite impossible to play at.

Z

Zooter – This refers to a variation of the flipper, which is typically bowled by leg-break bowlers. The ball is said to "zoot" along the ground and doesn't have much bounce. Some people believe this type of delivery is a myth created by Shane Warne for the purpose of confusing the opposing team.